NORTH RIDING

of one hundred years ago

MARKET PLACE, LEYBURN

CONCERT PARTY, SCARBOROUGH

NORTH RIDING

of one hundred years ago

DAVID GERRARD

ALAN SUTTON

First published in the United Kingdom in 1993 by
Alan Sutton Publishing Ltd · Phoenix Mill · Stroud · Gloucestershire

First published in the United States of America in 1993 by
Alan Sutton Publishing Inc · 83 Washington Street · Dover · NH 03820

British Library Cataloguing in Publication Data

A catalogue record for this book is available from the British Library

ISBN 0–7509–0292–2

Library of Congress Cataloging in Publication Data applied for

NORTON

Typeset in 11/13 Bembo.
Typesetting and origination by
Alan Sutton Publishing Limited.
Printed in Great Britain by
The Bath Press, Bath, Avon.

Preface

Anyone comparing a map of the old North Riding of Yorkshire with one of today's County of North Yorkshire immediately notices an important difference. When Local Authority boundaries were redrawn in 1974, the great industrial conurbation around the mouth of the River Tees was hived off to form part of an unconvincing entity called the County of Cleveland. At a stroke, the North Riding lost Middlesbrough, its largest town – 20 per cent of its population lived there – and its only sizeable industrial centre. Once again the county was what it had been until well into the nineteenth century – an almost exclusively rural society.

A hundred years ago there were a few small pockets of industrial activity, mostly mining for ironstone, lead or jet, and the fishing ports of Whitby and Scarborough were still significant contributors to the economy. But the overwhelming character of the county was of scattered communities living in small towns and villages, pursuing a way of life whose rhythms were orchestrated by the passing seasons.

In this collection of photographs and extracts from contemporary texts I have tried to harvest as abundant and diverse a crop as possible from the wealth of material available. Virtually everything in this book dates from the period between 1880 and the fateful watershed of 1914. The only exceptions are a small number of extracts recalling those years but written some time later. It is impossible in such a compilation to ignore one of the best books ever written about the North Riding: Canon J.C. Atkinson's mesmerizing account of his forty years as the Rector of Danby in the North York Moors, *Forty Years in a Moorland Parish*. Another major source is R.W.S. Bishop's much racier account of his years as a moorland doctor, *My Moorland Patients*, a highly enjoyable anthology of sharp and witty anecdotes. Most prolific of all

GREAT AYTON BRASS BAND

1

CRICKET FESTIVAL, HUTTON-LE-HOLE

Yorkshire writers of the time was Richard Blakeborough. A member of an old Yorkshire family, he was a working journalist who was happy to turn his hand to almost any subject (particularly if it had anything to do with sport). In the course of his working life he produced more than a hundred books as well as earning an occasional fee as a 'Society Humorist'.

In selecting the photographs I found that almost every picture of the North Riding of that time suffers in comparison with the towering genius of Whitby's resident photographer, Frank Meadow Sutcliffe. His beautifully composed, technically immaculate productions have now become classic images of the town. It is impossible not to include some of these, but I have tried to favour the less-familiar subjects.

In the preparation of this book I have benefited from the help of many people. In particular I would like to thank Duncan Allison and Caroline Alderson, Robin Cook, Michael Orr, Malcolm Race, Lillian Stephenson, Dan O'Sullivan, K.W. Scaife and R. Tee of Haxby Road School, York; Martin Watts and Hugh Templeman of the Ryedale Folk Museum, Hutton-le-Hole; Walkers Photographic Services, Scarborough and the staff of the North Yorkshire County Libraries at Richmond, Northallerton, Whitby and Scarborough.

David Gerrard
Constable Burton
Leyburn
North Yorkshire

Introduction

For the hardy middle-class travellers of late Victorian times the old North Riding of Yorkshire exercised a special attraction. It was remote, it was romantic – J.M.W. Turner's paintings had made sure of that – and much of it lay beyond the reach of lower-class 'railway excursionists'.

This last consideration was an important one. By the 1880s the incomparably detailed Ordnance Survey maps showed almost all of England covered by a cat's cradle of railway lines. But in England's fourth largest county the cobweb of snaking black lines revealed gaping holes where the formidable terrain of the Dales and Moors had discouraged the most optimistic of railway 'promoters'. True, a branch line did finally arrive at Richmond in 1846, but the company's shareholders baulked at the proposal to continue the route into the wild upper reaches of Swaledale.

It wasn't just the construction difficulties that stopped the Iron Horse in its tracks but also the fact that, even if the lines had been built, there was hardly anyone there to use them. For despite its 1.3 million acres, ranking among English counties just behind Devon, Lincolnshire and the West Riding, in a similar listing by population the North Riding only appeared in seventeenth place with less than 0.5 million inhabitants. Even that modest total gives a distorted view of the population density across the county, since 20 per cent of people were concentrated in the booming iron and steel town of Middlesbrough. A scarcely visible hamlet of four houses and twenty-five residents in 1801, a century later it had mushroomed into a vast, smoky conurbation of mills and docks sustaining a population of some one hundred thousand.

ELECTION CAMPAIGN, SCARBOROUGH

HERBERT SUMMERSON, SALTBURN BY THE SEA

The rest of the North Riding escaped the most awful consequences of this kind of Victorian industrial expansion. There were few towns of any size there, although the fashionable coastal resorts of Scarborough and Whitby flourished and Saltburn was created from virtually nothing into a demure sort of proto-Disneyland. The populations of Northallerton (the county town) and Richmond increased only minimally, or even declined, as some of their young men abandoned the somnolent market towns for the less-picturesque but much better-paying satanic mills of Middlesbrough.

The rest of this vast county remained a predominantly agricultural society, hostage to the fickle and often savage vagaries of the Yorkshire climate. It followed immemorial patterns of rural life established long before the Romans passed through the area, laying down their brutally straight roads arrowed towards the strategic forts of York, Newcastle and Carlisle. The earliest settlers had naturally seized the most fertile acres of the Vales of York, Mowbray and Pickering. Later arrivals, the Angles, Danes and Jutes, were forced to seek a livelihood in less generous locations, perhaps just a 'strip of

meadow beside the river', the Norse name in the eighth century for the Swaledale village of Muker.

When William the Conqueror's bureaucrats, compiling the Domesday Book, arrived in the North Riding in about 1080 they abandoned their usual meticulous accounting of 'caruscates', manors and 'ox-hides'. They dipped their quills and wrote off huge tracts of the country in a single word: 'wasteland'. This perception of a land where you could only expect to encounter 'discomfortable sheep and a tribe of demented peasants' (as one writer put it) endured well into the nineteenth century. As late as 1882 the compiler of Black's Guide to Yorkshire was solemnly advising his readers that 'only they who can endure fatigue, and philosophically content themselves with such accommodation as the somewhat primitive people can afford, should undertake to explore this remote part of Upper Swaledale'.

Such lugubrious warnings, far from deterring potential visitors to the North Riding, seem to have augmented their numbers. After all, at school Victorian children had been taught to honour the great British explorers of Africa and marvel at their superhuman endurance.

A visit to the more remote parts of Yorkshire necessarily involved a considerable degree of personal discomfort (a perennial topic of middle-class conversation), satisfied to a certain extent the pervading Victorian urge for 'discovery', but didn't leave you unfit for the drawing-room by rendering you unacceptably yellow and prostrate with malaria. And the scenery, of course, was magnificent. The 'wasteland' inscribed in the Domesday Book was now seen through the eyes of the fashionable painters of the Romantic Movement. Landscape that had been shunned as 'terrific' – in its old meaning of frightening – suddenly inspired the educated visitor to write rhapsodies celebrating its grandeur and the majesty of nature. Improved roads (and the few railway lines) were more prosaic reasons why the despised wildernesses of the North Riding suddenly blossomed into an aesthetically desirable place of resort.

This cultural U-turn had a minimal effect on the daily lives of most of the North Riding's working people. The drastic divide between rich and poor that tainted the unprecedented prosperity of nineteenth-century England was as stark here as anywhere in the country. Of the total population, 3 per cent possessed 30 per cent of the nation's wealth; 9 per cent classified as 'comfortable', held on to a further 14 per cent, while the remaining 88 per cent of English people ended up with an average annual income of £23.

Yorkshire farmers might have been more solicitous of their labourers' welfare than the mill-owners in the industrial towns – they certainly seem to have fed them better – but the average farm-worker's wage of 8s. a week (40p) provided only the barest necessities of food, clothing and housing.

In the industrial cities, the closely packed workforce could unite to demand fairer returns for their labour: in the scattered farmsteads of the North Riding, often miles apart, that kind of protest was impracticable. The only acceptable mode of dissent available to workmen and women was the Hiring Fair. Each year, at Michaelmas, they could take their badge of

CART AND CARRIAGE, SCARBOROUGH

employment (a crook for the shepherd, a mop for the maid) to one of the North Riding's market towns in search of a new employer. If they were lucky, they might be engaged by a less-tyrannical master, but even so, it was unlikely that their new quarterly wages would be any better than before. This harsh market-economy should have produced a docile breed of wage-slaves, humbly dependent on the grace and favour of their employers. Instead their isolation allowed individuality to flourish. As Dr Bishop, author of *My Moorland Patients*, observed:

Dwellers in towns, like stones in the pot-hole of a river-bed, have all their edges and peculiarities rounded off. In the country, on the other hand, there is so much elbow-room for everybody that individual eccentricities are accentuated, and the edges of character become sharp and rugged.

Such a society of sparsely educated men and women, not much given to writing, has left few personal records, but they continually force their way into the memoirs of their more leisured contemporaries. The references are sometimes patronizing, occasionally downright offensive, but equally often they reveal a genuine regard for the human dignity of their 'social inferiors'.

One such commentator was Canon J.C. Atkinson, Rector of Danby in the North Yorkshire Moors from the 1860s. In his classic work, *Forty Years in a Moorland Parish*, he gives a vivid picture of everyday life in his remote parish. But even he shared his contemporaries' acceptance of a society in which the nation's wealth was so randomly shared. At the bottom of the heap, according to Beerbohm Rowntree's study of poverty, one in four English people could afford 'no expenditure of any kind . . . beyond that which is absolutely necessary for the maintenance of merely physical efficiency'.

In one telling passage Canon Atkinson records that 'on occasion of some official inquiry as to the ways in which the working classes were housed', he accompanied the Commissioner to a village cottage where the whole family lived in a single room, with the hen-house as their next-door neighbour. In another farmhouse the beds had at least been partitioned off. 'But the partitions were in their construction and character merely such as those between stalls in a stable, except that no gentleman who cared for his horses would have tolerated them in his hunting or coaching stable.' But it becomes clear that Canon Atkinson is more distressed by the potential for immorality created by exposing young women to overcrowding of this kind, than by the workings of a social

5

MARKET PLACE, SCARBOROUGH

system that accepted such grinding poverty as part of the natural order of things.

There were, of course, many who did question the dominant philosophy expressed so succinctly in the popular hymn that invited both 'the rich man in his castle, the poor man at his gate' to join in celebrating God's blessings. The Rowntree family's chocolate factory in York was a model of enlightened industrial relations. In Middlesbrough, Lady Bell, the wife of a leading mill-owner, wrote a compassionate book, *At the Works*, detailing the degrading conditions endured by the workers and followed this up with practical help.

'Merrie England' the North Riding was not. But markets, fairs, weddings, the itinerant bands, the pierrots on the beach and the seasonal rituals of the May Pole or the Christmas Carol Singers seemed all the brighter for the dull, back-breaking routine that surrounded them. Funerals, too, were major social events for the poor, 'a good sending-off' being a matter of deep family pride. And, without subscribing to the romantic view of a nation peopled by 'sturdy British yeomen'

and 'a stout-hearted peasantry', in many ways it *was* a more attractive society than our own. The internal combustion engine hadn't wrought its havoc: it was still possible for children to play and their parents to stand gossiping in the middle of a main road. Crime, in the countryside at least, was a minor problem; new buildings still respected the human scale and architects still sought to attract the eye rather than repel it. Individual traders – blacksmiths, tailors, cobblers, bakers, butchers – all provided a personal service, while a succession of travelling salesmen offering an eclectic range of goods and services (bottle corks, fairings, knife and scissor-grinding, even the latest fashions) provided welcome diversions.

The novelist L.P. Hartley opened his book *The Go-Between* with the haunting words 'The past is a foreign country: they do things differently there.' It's a country we can now only visit with the help of those who wrote about it, or photographed it, at the time. I hope that this selection of their words and their images will evoke an authentic sense of this far-off, vanished country.

NORTH RIDING

of one hundred years ago

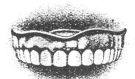

SHOOTING PARTY, SWAINBY

INVASION OF THE GROUSE SHOOTERS

A great day in my young life was the opening of the grouse shooting season in August. Twenty or thirty beaters were roped in to drive the birds and we older boys were included. The whole village was agog as magnificent horse-drawn shooting brakes, cooks and valets rolled into view.

Generally the sportsmen took over the village inn and their retainers were boarded out, but one year, for some reason I cannot recall, our house was taken over. Where we slept I've no idea – I can only remember that hamper upon hamper of the choicest victuals and cases of champagne and choice wines were stacked upon our sideboard, and feasting went on for two or three days. By that time the grouse had had enough – what was left of them.

It was heavy going for the beaters, mostly through knee-high ling. A break was called at mid-day for lunch which, for the beaters, was invariably rabbit pie. The party, of course, feasted on the contents of hampers brought up by pony to the moor. For quantity, however, they would be well beaten by the beaters, for their job was strenuous and provided a great appetite.

To provide the rabbit pie I once accompanied the gamekeeper a few nights previous to the beat, when about thirty 'bunnies' were shot and carried to our house to be converted into pies. There must have been something to go along with them, for a rabbit pie is a poor dish by itself.

In a day or two traces of the invasion would gradually disappear, though in our house the aroma of our visitors' stay remained for days.

C. T. Maltby

TIM HAYGARTH THE POACHER

As we walked along the road beneath its steep slope we overtook Tim Haygarth, the most inveterate poacher of our district. He is a most interesting character, and knows more about bird, beast, and plant life in our valleys than probably any two other men put together. But Tim keeps his own counsel; only a good-sized silver key will induce him to unlock his secrets to any but a few prime favourites.

Although Tim has several times got into trouble, his depth and cunning are such that, in forty-nine cases out of fifty, he is able to 'go one better' than those in authority. One cold, foggy November night Tim had just caught an eighteen-pound salmon when he was surprised by the river watcher. Promptly did Tim and his prize disappear into the stream, and in a deep hole just below the bank he stood up to his neck in water for fully fifty minutes! The watcher meanwhile searched for him high and low. At the end of that time he gave up the search and proceeded on his beat, thinking that, after all, he must have been mistaken, despite the fact that he had twice been within a couple of yards of his quarry. Tim was laid up for some weeks after this episode with a bad attack of rheumatism.

YARM ANGLING ASSOCIATION

On another occasion two farmers were caught by the gamekeepers when they had just drawn a twenty-six pound fish from the stream. So intent were they on their prize, that it was not until one of the watchers placed his hand on the shoulder of one of them that they were aware of their presence.

'My word, Postlethwaite, that's much too fine a salmon not to know the weight of,' said the watcher. 'Let us take it to the police-station and have it weighed,' he continued, and with that he marched the men and the fish off into the town.

Tim, as is his wont when not otherwise engaged, was standing in the market-place with his hands in his pockets. Noticing what was up as the four men passed, he immediately got his own 'tackle' and set off to the river, knowing well that after the capture the keepers would require some little refreshment at the inn before setting out again on their rounds. Tim cleared three salmon out of the identical pool where the others had been caught, and, what is more, got safely home with them unmolested. We walked some little distance with Tim, and I casually remarked to him, àpropos of the above incident:

'Mustn't Postlethwaite have felt dropped upon when the watchers caught him in January last?'

He just looked slyly at me out of the corner of his eye, and remarked:

'Silly fellow, he shouldn't do such things.'

P.H. Lockwood

OLD PETER THE GAMEKEEPER, SWAINBY

CHILDREN'S CORNER, SCARBOROUGH

ALIEN CHILDREN EVERYWHERE

Though the moorlanders were jealous enough about their sheep and stock rights, and quarrelled incessantly about them, they never seemed to be jealous of their women folk. There were alien children everywhere, and everybody knew who their fathers were except the children themselves. I was repeatedly asked by the mothers whom these children resembled, and they were evidently very proud to enlighten me. I remember once being asked before a room full of people, by the mother of a farmer's wife, herself the wife of a highly respected farmer, who her daughter was the 'spit and image of.' I knew of course to whom she was alluding but affected ignorance, and received a sound rating for my dullness. The girl was a squire's daughter.

R.W.S. Bishop

SATURDAY BATH NIGHT

. . . we used to love Saturday bath night, because we didn't have to go to bed so early. We were only bathed on the Saturday: you weren't splashing in water all t'time, as you are today. Of course, there was no bathroom. Water was boiled in the side-boiler, and we had a big settle; us four children used to sit on there in a row, and Mother used to fetch this tin bath and bath us all in the same water. She started with the youngest first, and it was pretty clear then, but it was getting a bit thick when it got to me!

Because, of course, there was no running water: you hadn't a tap to turn on. All that water was to cart from our pasture.

We had a spring of lovely water there: it sparkled when it came out o'limestone, and it was as clear as a bell. But it was hard water: you had to put an awful lot o' soap on to get a lather with it, it was that hard. It all was to carry to the house in buckets, or sometimes me father would take his back-can, what he fetched his milk in, and carry that filled up, so's we hadn't to go for any more. Then it was all to heat in side-boiler. That was why Mother would always wash herself in the afternoon: she couldn't wash in the morning, because there was no hot water in a morning. . . .

So you didn't waste hot water, no! And on bath night, when we'd all had wir baths, all wir underwear went into bath-water to steep, and then 'twas carted away and left in that water seeping 'til Monday. You never washed anything on a Sunday, you know. Sundays *was* Sundays, and we couldn't even bring wir games out, on a Sunday.

Maggie Joe Chapman

EASTER WEEK CUSTOMS

The days in Holy Week are familiarly known as Collop Monday, Pancake Tuesday, Frutas or Fritters Wednesday, Bloody Thursday.

> An' Lang Friday 'at's nivver deean,
> Seea lig i' bed whahl Seterdaay neean.

The usual menu for the week is still pretty much as it was. Collops of bacon and fried eggs on Monday. Pancakes served with either treacle or lemon-juice and sugar on Tuesday.

CRAB WHEEL, SUTTON

Frutas, or fritters, made from a light kind of tea-cake paste, only much richer in fruit and fried either in lard or butter, on Wednesday; and, with many of humble degree, black puddings on Thursday. Whilst on Friday, fast is kept on any frutas which may have been spared from Wednesday's feast, and there always is a very considerable helping left over.

Paste-egg or Troll-egg Day, is now celebrated on Easter Monday, but in days past Easter Day and Paste-Egg Day were one. At the present time the last five Sundays of Lent and Easter Day are still called Tid, Mid, Miseray, Carlin', and Paum, an' Paste-egg Day. There is some uncertainty as to what Tid and Mid mean, but there can be no doubt that Miseray is a corruption of Miserere, the commencement of one of the psalms ordered to be read during Lent. The whole of the names, however, take us back to mediaeval times, and though some are inclined to think that Tid means 'Te Deum' and Mid 'Mid Lent,' it seems to me careful research will in time give a more plausible solution. Carling Sunday is still observed in many places, grey peas fried with bacon or in butter being a well-known dish on that day, many even carrying a goodly store about in paper bags. At Great Ayton, and in many parts of Cleveland, Carling Sunday is still fully observed. The same is equally true of Palm Sunday, or, as it is called, 'Paum Sunda,' catkins, or lambs' tails, as they are universally designated, being carried in the hand, thrust in the buttonhole, or worn in the hat, whilst many a mantel-piece and ornament is often tastefully decorated with the same. From noon on Easter Day to noon the following day, an old custom which is now only kept up in remote villages, but which was quite general throughout the riding when I was a lad, was that of one or more young fellows seizing a female and forcibly pulling off her shoe, sometimes both, laces being no protection. These were held in bondage until a fine was paid. This very rough proceeding was formerly known as 'buckle-snatching,' the old name for the theft during the days when buckles were worn. However, if the lads had their good time from the Sunday to Monday's noon, the lasses did not fail to retaliate from that time until noon on Tuesday. From any hidden corner or doorway, out they rushed, and rarely failed to snatch either a hat, whip, stick, handkerchief, or something, they were not particular what, or to scratching either, generally managing to recuperate themselves for any losses of the day previous. On Easter Monday the bairns hie themselve to some field and roll or troll their hard-boiled eggs dyed in many colours; this lasts until the egg is broken, when the youngsters feed upon the contents.

Richard Blakeborough

12

GOLDEN JUBILEE FEAST, GREAT AYTON

A Jubilee Tea

17th May, 1897. 'Ordered that, on the 60th anniversary of the Queen's accession to the throne, 1/- [5p] be paid to outdoor relief recipients and 6d [2½p] to each child. Inmates to have a special tea with double allowance of Bread, Tea, Sugar and Milk, to finish off with one buttered hot cake each.'

27th June, 1887. 'Ordered that George Easterley, a pauper, employed as a nurse in the Male Infirmary, be allowed one ounce of Rum daily, the Medical Officer having recommended that allowance.'

Minutes of the Pickering Workhouse Guardians

'Affected by the Pauper Taint'

Children. – The number of children in York Workhouse on January 1, 1901 was 70. Although theoretically they are forbidden to mix with the adult paupers, it is very difficult in a Workhouse strictly to enforce this regulation. When old enough they are sent to the ordinary elementary schools in York, where they hold their own fairly well with other children.

It is to be regretted that so many children are brought up in the Workhouse, as they can hardly fail to become affected by the pauper taint. A certain number of children under the care of the Guardians are, however, boarded out, or placed in certified homes, and at the time of writing an effort is being made to send more of those now in the Workhouse to orphanages and other certified homes for children. Although this course presents some advantages over bringing them up in the Workhouse, it would be undoubtedly much better if they could be dealt with on the scattered homes system so successfully followed at Sheffield, Leeds, and Bradford.

As soon as the children leave school, the Guardians obtain positions for them. Most of the girls go to service, and the boys to farms or to other situations where they can 'live in'.

B. Seebohm Rowntree

'Very Mean' – but not at the Table

First place I went out to, at Bainbridge, the master had a hump on his back, and he was supposed to be very greedy, very mean. But this night, when I hadn't been there long, there was bannocks on table – scones, you might call 'em – bread, butter, and jam or cheese, whichever you wanted. And master came in from front room, and said:

'Had thee supper, lad?'

'No, I'm just going to get it.'

Then he turned to t'housekeeper (she was a fresh housekeeper, she hadn't been there long) and he says:

MARKET PLACE, LEYBURN.

'That's no good to a growing lad. He wants beef, bacon and eggs.' And he got carving knife, and he went into t'pantry, and he fetched the biggest chunk o' beef I'd ever seen: it was half-an-inch thick.

'Eat that, lad. That sweet stuff's no good to you. That's no good to work on.' He didn't believe i' sweet stuff. He once caught me eating a sweet: somebody had gone past and given me a toffee.

'What's tha eating, lad?'

'Nay, just a toffee.'

'Han't had plenty o' breakfast? Gan and tell th' housekeeper tha wants some more. Tha wants nowt wi' that stuff!'

And back I had to go. Oh, in his own way he was very mean – but not at the table!

Bob Metcalfe

A FREE PHEASANT FOR LUNCH

There were no less than four Paddisons in the School in those days – three brothers and a cousin. The youngest brother was my especial pal. I remember walking over Leyburn Moors with him one half term holiday. It was our habit in those days to spend this whole holiday in long walks – twenty, thirty and even forty miles long – to Reeth and back, to Askrigg and back or to Hawes and back. On this occasion Joe said to me suddenly, 'Have you any money?' 'I have a shilling,' I said. 'But I have nothing at all,' said he. A shilling was hardly an adequate sum to provide lunch for two hungry youngsters walking all day in the keen Yorkshire air. We looked at each other in consternation. Suddenly a wounded pheasant limped across the road. Joe knocked it over with a stone, and we took it along with us. When we got to Askrigg we knocked at a cottage door. 'We have a shilling and a pheasant,' we said, 'If we give them you, will you give us lunch?' 'Yes, certainly,' said the cottager; and she did a very good lunch.

John Stuart Hodgson

VILLAGE 'MARKSMEN'

Forty-five years ago it was not unusual for a farmer to be unable to read or write, sometimes both. The then tenant of far the largest farm in the parish was compelled to 'make his mark' for this reason, and so was my nearest neighbour, the tenant of one of Lord Downe's largest farms; and it was a very common thing for the parish clerk, who held the office of parish schoolmaster as well (and so was 'qualified to know'), to say to me when I was preparing to register the newly solemnised marriage that one or more of the parties – sometimes all four, or the newly wedded pair and the witnesses – were 'marksmen'; in other words, could not write their names.

J.C. Atkinson

14

SWAINBY, FROM THE BRIDGE

THE DOG-WHIPPER'S HOUSE

There are two of the old-fashioned, as well as old, cottages, once the rule in the district, still remaining in one part of the parish. In one of these, when I first came, the Dog-whipper [Willy Richardson], his brother (and successor), and their sister lived together. The hut contained one room (with a floor sunk beneath the level of the ground), of perhaps four yards square, and no pretence at a separate room for the woman, there being no loft even. In the other, much the same in point of area and arrangement, lived a married couple with their family; and when the Dog-whipper family died out, their cottage was occupied by another married couple and their offspring. The united population of these two one-roomed, loftless dens at one time reached the trifling total of twenty-three souls!

J.C. Atkinson

DISCRETION OF THE DOG-WHIPPER

Forty years ago the 'Dog-whipper' was still an institution in this dale. Auld Willy Richardson was then the hereditary holder of the office, his father having been dog-whipper before him; and when Willy himself died, the office, the honour, and the insignia passed to his brother John. For the office was by no means one without outward signs and tokens

of its existence. The office-holder held also a whip, and whenever he was on duty the whip was *en évidence*.

Poor old Willy, the first dog-whipper of my acquaintance, was a little man of about five feet four, with legs that were hardly a pair, and which it would have been slander to call straight or well shapen; and, as was natural perhaps, he shambled in his gait. His usual garb on the Sunday was an ancient drab coat, cut – if a tailor had ever been concerned in the making of it – after the fashion described as that of Dominie Sampson's, with broad skirts falling quite below the knee. There were side-pockets in it, opening just upon the hip; capacious and with a sort of suggestiveness about them that they were not simply meant to contain sundries, but were put to such a use by wont and custom. On Sundays, and days when a 'burying' was to be – for Willy was sexton also, and kept the depth of his graves religiously to under three feet – the short handle of the whip he bore reposed in the right-hand pocket, but the lainder and lash hung outside; the latter, inasmuch as the bearer's stature was not great, trailing on the ground.

Willy was valorous in the execution of his duty, although he may sometimes have seen occasion for the exercise of a wise discretion. I knew of two such instances. In one the intrusive dog was made slowly to recede before the duly-armed official, who was fairly well able to command the whole interspace between the pews which runs the length of the church; but when it came to turning round the corner and backing towards the door, the dog did not see the expediency of the

15

WHEELGATE, MALTON

desired course quite so clearly as Willy did; and so, having more room in the crossing in which to attain the necessary impetus, he made a bolt for it, aiming at the archway presented by the dog-whipper's bow-legs. But the archway proved to be less than the dog had assumed it to be; and, in consequence, after riding backwards for a pace or two, poor old Willy came backwards to the pavement, and to grief besides. The dog on the other occasion was more resolute, or else less accommodating; for he met all Willy's advances with a steady refusal to budge an inch in a backward direction. Willy persevered; the dog growled. Willy showed his whip; the dog showed his teeth; and the teeth having a more persuasive look about them than the whip, the man gave way and the dog did not.

J.C. Atkinson

BEARERS OF THE COFFIN

. . . the coffin is never borne on the shoulders of the bearers, as is most customary elsewhere. So far as it is 'carried by hand' at all – which, from the distance of the church from all the constituents of the population, is very little, usually only from a few yards outside the churchyard-gate to the trestles set to support it in the western part of the nave of the church – it is carried by the aid of towels knotted together and passed under the coffin, the ends on either side being held by the bearers, six in number (or three pairs). And as regards the bearers, the usage was so consistent and so steadfast that there would be no impropriety in speaking of it as 'the rule.' Thus a single

woman was borne by six single young women, a single young man by six of his compeers, a married woman by married women, and so on all through. Nay, it is no unusual sight even yet to see the child carried by six children, varying according to the sex of the dead child. In the case of the young unmarried woman, moreover, some peculiarities of costume were always to be observed about the bearers. Their dress was not all unrelieved black. White sashes or scarfs were customarily worn, and white gloves always. Much of this remains still, but the observance in such matters is hardly so religious as it used to be.

J.C. Atkinson

YORKSHIRE BREEZES

I have been often at great heights on the Alps in rough weather, and have seen strong gusts of storm in the plains of the south. But to get full expression of the very heart and the meaning of wind, there is no place like a Yorkshire moor. I think Scottish breezes are thinner, very bleak and piercing, but not substantial.

If you lean on them they will let you fall, but one may rest against a Yorkshire breeze as one would on a quickset hedge. I shall not soon forget, – having had the good fortune to meet a vigorous one on an April morning, between Hawes and Settle, just on the flat under Whernside,– the vague sense of wonder with which I watched Ingleborough stand without rocking.

John Ruskin

OLD SCARBOROUGH HARBOUR

A MOONSTRUCK CREATURE

It was my duty as a poor-law medical officer to certify all those who, by their inability to pay the higher charges of a lunatic asylum, became *ipso facto* paupers, and if I had certified all those I considerd to be insane I would have locked up a good proportion of the countryside.

One of these moonstruck creatures had already been in an asylum once for a short time, and the story went about that on this occasion, when he arrived with a half-baked relation of the same name at the institution, the doctors had been in so much doubt as to which was the lunatic, that they nearly succeeded in locking up the wrong man. There is no need to describe his appearance, beyond stating that he was the exact facsimile of Uncle Sam Slick with his long goatee beard. He was the terror of a small hamlet in the middle of the moorland, consisting of two or three farms, seven or eight cottages, and a chapel, and in particular of his faithful wife, who was of course a cousin. He kept a small store, played the harmonium at the chapel, had five children, and £500 in the

bank. I was very sorry for his wife, and most reluctant to put him under restraint, because I knew the £500 would soon melt in asylum charges. Moreover, I was by no means sure he was really mad. He puzzled me very much and gave me a good deal of trouble. At times when he was excited by a full moon and unusually naughty, I would, as a measure of precaution, have him carefully watched by his neighbours. Against one of these he nursed a small private grievance. One day this man and another farmer were sitting quietly by him, when he suddenly struck a most vicious blow at the obnoxious neighbour, which missed its mark and landed heavily on the stomach of the other man – winding him, and nearly finishing him off. He apologised most profusely to the latter, explaining that he had intended the blow for his companion. There was too much method here, I thought.

To frighten his wife he used to rush furiously at the sides of bacon hung up in his kitchen, with a big carving knife, stabbing them all over. . . .

On another occasion he got up in the middle of the night, and after very quietly dressing, got the carving knife and

17

BROMPTON

narrowly scrutinised his wife's face to see if she were asleep. Satisfied on this point, he carefully packed in a butter basket the best china tea-service, carried it a mile on to the moor and then unpacked it, leaving it among the heather covered with bracken.

His wife had cautiously followed at a distance to watch his proceedings, and a few days afterwards, when the moon had passed the quarter, brought back the tea-service, and restored it to its proper place without comment from her spouse. . . .

Finally, one day he took off every rag of clothing, and in stark nakedness and in anything but his right mind, attended to the demands of his customers, to their great consternation. I am sure they sought in vain for the human form divine in his scarecrow of a body. Although it was very hot weather, there was no excuse for this kind of behaviour; so I had him put under lock and key again.

R.W.S. Bishop

No 'Tea-boily' for the Workers

The people I started with . . . were very frugal savers, and by the time he was in his sixties they'd saved enough to take a bit o' land: but by the time he was about sixty-eight, the 'miner's cough' had got him, and he couldn't do owt. So they hired me at five shilling a week.

And that family, they had 'tea-boily'. The tea that had been left from tea-table was warmed up with a drop of milk, and poured onto some bread. But they never would let *me* have any. For the simple reason that they were frightened that I went boastfully up into the village, and said I'd had a special supper o' tea-boily. And tea-boily, you see, was a stigma of absolute poverty, and I hadn't to have it, in case I set a rumour going up in the town, that I was fed on tea-boily. Because I'll

give them their due, they fed me as good, or rather better, nor they fed themselves. But they *wouldn't* give me tea-boily. *They* were used to it, and they liked it: they used to put a bit o' sugar to it, and it was the kind o' supper they really enjoyed. But they wouldn't have it said they fed their farm servants on it.

Kit Calvert

A Postcard from Brompton

dear Aunty emmie,

I like the coat very much it just fits me. You must look well at this Post Card you will see Willie Harold and Ruth on it we saw it in a shop window we thought you would like it we will send you another soon from

Grace, 5 April 1905

'A Tenacious 'Hob'

We cannot leave the subject of 'Hob' without relating the familiar and amusing account of his persistent attachment to a Farndale farmer. 'Hob' was so troublesome a visitor, and so vexed and annoyed him, that he determined to leave his present abode and seek some other. As he journeyed on his way with all his household goods in a cart, he met a neighbour, who accosted him with the words, 'I see you are flitting' – 'Aye, we're flutting,' came from 'Hob' out of the churn; so the farmer seeing he was carrying his troublesome familiar with him, concluded he might as well return to his old home.

Two Sunday School Teachers

'BIDDEN TO T'BURIAL'

As soon after the breath had left the body as was possible, the next day at the latest – often the same day, if the person had died early – the person whose professional name was 'the bidder,' went round from house to house among those who were to be 'bidden to t' burial,' to 'warn' them that the burial was fixed for such and such a day, and to add, 'and so and so' – naming the principal friend or friends of the deceased – 'expect you at ten o'clock in the morning.' The 'minister' was always among the first to be bidden. Sometimes when the dead person had been long in the place, had borne parochial office, and had won the goodwill and respect of all the neighbours, or if he was a man with numerous relations and connections (a very common case), or for whom general sympathy had been aroused, these invitations might be numbered, not merely by the score, but by the hundred. I have myself counted more than three hundred seated in the church on at least four, if not five, different occasions. And the rule is, and, still more, was, that the preponderating majority of these 'went to the burial' at the house where the corpse lay, beginning at ten o'clock and continuing to drop in, according to convenience or distance to be traversed, throughout the morning and afternoon till it became time to 'lift the body' and make a start for the church.

And all these were fed – entertained, rather – at the house of mourning, if it chanced to be that of one of the principal inhabitants. All day long, in relays of from a dozen up to a score, according to the dimensions of the reception-room, the hungry host came streaming in, until all had been 'served.' Those who had been the first to enter went and sat about wherever they could find seats, whether in the house or outside, or in the farm premises, or at some neighbour's, smoking (not without the necessary 'wet,' it might be) and chatting, as on any other occasion when friends and acquaintances were wont to meet. The last part of the entertainment, at least in the later days of the old practice, was to hand round on salvers or trays glasses of wine and small round cakes of the crisp sponge description, of which most of the guests partook.

J.C. Atkinson

AN INKLING OF HEAVEN

The village artist was dying; he had painted three out of the four village signs, he had executed the scrollwork for every church decoration for years past, and there was in his house an imitation marble mantlepiece, which he had yearned to show every one. The clergyman was about to leave him, but before doing so, asked if he should pray. 'Aye, aye,' said the dying man, 'and ez mebbe this'll be t' last tahm 'at ya will pray foor ma, Ah s'u'd be glad if ya'd mention 'at Ah's a good hand at decorating; it'll mebbe help yan a bit.'

Old Matthew was a well-known character. For years both he and his old dame lived in a little cottage near Newton-under-Rosebery. When on his death-bed, a lady, after reading

SANDSEND FROM LYTHE BANK

to him, said, 'And after all I have read and told you, Matthew, heaven is more beautiful than you can possibly imagine; you might lie and call to mind all the beautiful things you have either seen or dreamt of, and even then you would not have the least idea what heaven is like.' To say the least, she was somewhat surprised when the old man, gently patting her hand, said in a whisper, 'Ya mebbe deean't knaw 'at Ah yance seed Leeds pantomine; that gave yan a inkling.' N.B. – The Yorkshire people always pronounce 'pantomime' as spelt above.

Richard Blakeborough

'BLACK, BLIND AND SINISTER' LEECHES

Scenes of childhood end abruptly with the death of my Father. In the Winter of my ninth year, he was taken ill with pneumonia; the house became muted and silent. Mrs. Walker, the nurse from one of the cottages by Peacock's farm, whom I have not mentioned before, but who had attended my Mother in all her confinements, was called in; and our cousin the Doctor came from Kirby daily. He and my Father were fast friends, and when the illness became critical, all his energies were devoted to the saving of this precious life. But in vain. Rheumatic fever developed. The air of anguish in every one, my Mother's tearful eyes – these were obvious even to us children. One day leeches were brought, and stood in a glass jar on a shelf in the dairy. They were black, blind and sinister. But then we were taken away. I went to Howkeld, and one night I suffered intolerable ear-ache, so that I cried aloud, and was poulticed with onions. The pain had gone in the morning, but by my Aunt's tears I knew that my Father was dead. The next day I was driven back to the Farm. The blinds were drawn, everywhere it was very still, and dark. We were taken upstairs to say good-bye to my dead Father. The cold wintry light came evenly through the open slats of the venetian blind. My Father lay on the bed, sleeping, as he always did, with his arms on the coverlet, straight down each side of his body. His beautiful face was very white, except for the red marks on his temples, where the leeches had clung. I was told to kiss that face; it was deadly cold, like the face of Little Meg's mother.

I felt stunned, but could not comprehend my loss, nor the grief of those about me. I moved away in the unnatural stillness, walking in a living sleep. Downstairs candles were burning on a table laden with cold meat and cakes. Then we all drove to Kirkdale, slowly over the frozen flint roads, and there a grave was ready dug at the east end of the Church, by the side of Mariana's.

Herbert Read

LATE FOR THEIR OWN FUNERAL

Necessarily when there were such numbers of friends and relations to be fed, and such scant accommodation as cramped space in the kitchen, as well as at the board, entailed, there was great loss of time, and often exceeding unpunctuality in the starting, and, much more, the arrival at the churchyard of the funeral cortege. Once in my predecessor's time the arrival did not take place until after dark, and the service in the church – which is near no house at all save one, and that is a third of a mile distant – had to be read by the light of a tallow dip, procured after some delay, and the grave-side service by the wavering, flickering light of the same held in the sexton's hand.

J.C. Atkinson

WEST AYTON

PRESENT AT THE BIRTH

An old medical friend told me of the case of a man who was almost insanely jealous of his wife, and insisted on being present at her confinement. He had approached four doctors in turn who all refused his odd request. My friend effected a compromise. The husband sat throughout his wife's ordeal, with his back to the bed under a kind of awning specially constructed for the occasion. Fortunately Dame Nature was very kind and no complications arose.

R.W.S. Bishop

GOOD LUCK FROM A CAUL

When a child is born with a mask or caul over its head, good luck will follow it all the days of its life, always provided the caul is properly preserved. There is some rite in the preservation of such, the details of which I have not been able to obtain. Speaking to one old dame, she said to me that she did not rightly know what they did in such cases, none of her children having been fortunate enough to be so distinguished at their birth. This much, however, she did know, that some just dried such a covering by laying it between two layers of muslin, but – and to give her own words – 'Ther's other some 'at 'ev a straange carrying on wi' sike leyke; they lap it roond t' Bahble an' deea summat, bud Ah deean't knaw what, bud Ah can git ti knaw foor ya.' That cannot be now; she has crossed the borderland. That such cauls or masks were held in high esteem at one time, is proved by the high prices paid for

TWO SISTERS, WEST AYTON

ON THE SANDS, SCARBOROUGH

them, not because they had belonged to people of note or high degree, but because they possessed the power to ward off many evils which might assail the possessor. Sailors even to-day set great store by them: they act as a charm, saving the possessor from drowning in case of a wreck. These veils were much prized by witches, and great was the evil they could work should such ever come into their possession, hence the necessity of using all precautions against their loss.

Richard Blakeborough

MARIANA AT THE GRANGE

One day my Father brought a delightful toy back from Northallerton: it was a small musical box which played 'For there's nae luck about the house'. But my Mother, perhaps then, or perhaps shortly afterwards, when there was sufficient cause, thought the tune was ominous. My only sister was a baby then, between two and three years old. Our Farm was called the Grange, and though it had no moat, this daughter was christened Mariana. Perhaps that too was ominous, for a sad song goes by her name. Mariana was fair as sunlight, and smiled to the tinkle of the musical box. And that is all I remember of her, for that Spring I was suddenly sent away. A few days later my Aunt told me that Mariana had become an angel, and the next time we went to Kirkdale I was taken to see the unmeaning mound that covered her body.

Herbert Read

'FOR THE INTERMENT OF A CHILD'

	1st class	2nd class
For the interment of a child under seven years of age	10s. 9d.	4s. 6d.
For the interment of an adult	16s. 6d.	6s. 6d.
Non-residents and burials at a time not fixed by the Minister	double above fees	
Interment at expense of township ...	5s. 6d.	
Interment of a still born child... ...	3s. 6d.	
For introduction of an upright head-stone	7s. 6d.	
For the freehold of a single grave space	£5	
For planting a grave with flowers (per annum in advance)	2s. 6d.	

The depths of graves for persons sixteen years of age and above shall be 7 ½ feet and for persons under 16 years of age 6 feet. Above charges are exclusive of any dues or fees payable to the Incumbent or Clerk.

Eston Parish Burial Charges

THE BUTTERTUBS PASS, SWALEDALE

A 'VEXATIOUS AND DAMAGING NUISANCE'

That this Council is of the opinion that all Motor Vehicles should be in some measure further taxed, and that a grant from the revenue so derived should be made towards the expenses of watering the roads in every district, with a view to reducing the vexatious and damaging nuisance caused by the dust.

Guisborough Council Resolution, 1906

ROADS ARE 'HORRIBLY LOOSE & STONY'

Roads. – The roads are of varying degrees of merit, according to the nature of the country in which they occur. In the great central plain the surface of the main routes is excellent, but many of the by-lanes – especially in the neighbourhood of *Easingwold* – are horribly loose and stony. In the W. dales ordinary traffic is practically confined to the bottoms of the valleys, and the mountain tracks and passes that traverse the ridges are almost impassably rough and precipitous. Among the E. moorlands the only really passable road is the one that runs up *Bilsdale* from *Helmsley* to *Stokesley*, for even the old coaching-road from *Pickering* to *Whitby* is now seldom used, and is frightfully stony on the section from Saltergate to *Sleights*. Here and there, of course, in the bottoms of the

valleys are short lengths of tolerable surface; but most of the roads are mere winding farm lanes, or rutty and sandy moorland tracks. For cyclists, in fact, the E. moorlands are far less practicable than the W. fells, where at any rate *Wensleydale, Teesdale,* and *Swaledale* may be comfortably traversed from end to end.

J.E. Morris

A DRIVE THROUGH THE BUTTERTUBS PASS

Hawes lies on the other side of the valley at the foot of the blue hills, in a lovely position beside the Ure; and when we have reached a point exactly opposite to it we turn sharply up a steep pitch on the right, with a splendid panoramic view of mountains on the left as we climb.

This is the beginning of the Buttertubs Pass. From this point onwards, till the road plunges down into Swaledale, the surface is composed more or less of loose stones. The stiffest upward gradients we shall have to encounter are within a mile or two of this spot, for the wild part of the pass – the real moorland – is comparatively level, and by the time we reach the actual Buttertubs we are already running down. This is the climax – this point where the downward gradient begins – for here suddenly the solid earth seems to fall away from us: here suddenly the rough and narrow road

RAVENSCAR STATION

is no longer lying across the far-stretching moorland, but is hanging high upon the hillside, clinging upon the extremest edge of a gulf which drops dizzily into a blue sea of shadows. Thus it clings for miles. Beyond the chasm the bare hillside rises again above our heads in magnificent curves, glowing with colour, and cleft here and there into purple gorges. Slightly above the road on the left are the Buttertubs, strange crater-like hollows of unplumbed depth, appearing at intervals beside us, with sharp rocks bristling through the grass at their mouths. As we slowly descend, the hills of Swaledale rise before us like a wall blocking the defile; and presently a gate across the road shows that we are near the world again.

Truly this is one of the runs that are unforgettable. To be among these savage heights and depths, these heaving waves of desolate moor, to have these solitudes above us and these blue shadows so far below us, is to know something of 'the strong foundations of the earth.' It is with a feeling of anti-climax that we close the gate behind us, and, on a precipitous gradient and no surface worth mentioning, steer slowly down into Swaledale.

As we cautiously make our way over the stones of this very trying lane, we are confronted with rather a startling notice board: 'No Road.' It seems a little late to tell us that now: they might have mentioned it before we crossed the pass! Then it dawns upon us that the amateur hand that

traced the letters had sloped the board in the wrong direction. It is really meant to face down the valley, for the discouragement of those who might stray up from Swaledale, ignorant of the pass.

Mrs Rodolph Stawell

DIFFERENCE BETWEEN A FIRST- AND THIRD-CLASS TICKET

A rather good story is told of a stranger journeying to a far distant dale in Yorkshire. On arrival at the railway terminus he proceeded to engage a seat in a conveyance plying to his destination. Asked if he required a first-, second-, or third-class ticket, he took a first-class, though not a little mystified by the request. This mystification became annoyance when at the appointed time all crowded into the conveyance without any distinction of class. He naturally thought he had been 'had.' However, after a five-mile run on the level, the driver pulled up at the foot of a tremendously long steep hill. 'First-class passengers,' he directed, 'sit still, second-class passengers get out and walk, third-class passengers shove up behind.'

R.W.S. Bishop

SCARBOROUGH BEACH

SAVING THE YOUNG WOMEN OF SCARBOROUGH

My grandmother Sitwell's favourite virtue was, perhaps, that known as Charity. But hers was of a peculiar kind.

She had never *really* succeeded in *liking* St. Mary Magdalen, who had, to be frank, a rather horrid Roman Catholic air about her. And yet she felt bound to accept her, in a cold manner, owing to the passages in the New Testament. It was, perhaps, owing to this forced acceptance on my grandmother's part, that she determined to wrap equally deplorable young persons in an unescapable charity.

Therefore she, and a Suffragan Bishop, with a frost-bitten appearance like something on a cheap Christmas card, would, on hot summer evenings at Scarborough, make sorties together in her barouche, driven by her old coachman Hill. Encircling the town they would surround and capture any young woman who appeared to them to be unsuitably dressed and in a deplorable 'state of joyosity' as John Knox called it.

Aided by Hill, my grandmother and the Bishop would seize these unfortunates, and decant them into a red brick house known as The Home, where, supervised by Sister Edith, the matron, a bursting woman like an advertisement for tomatoes on a railway station, they earned their living by tearing our laundry to shreds every week.

It was one of the rules of The Home that every kidnapped young person must, immediately on her arrival, be given a bath under the supervision of Sister Edith. They were then encased in twill nightgowns, like strait waistcoats. Next morning, they were forced to put on the Home uniform, hideous navy blue coats and skirts, and boots like those worn by policemen in years past. With this attire they wore shapeless navy blue felt hats.

Edith Sitwell

SUPERSTITIONS OF THE EDUCATED

I have met with any number of educated, cultured people who devoutly believe that suffering the sun to shine freely upon a fire in the ordinary grate puts it out; that setting a poker vertically up against the fire grate in front of it, causes the smouldering, nearly extinct fire to burn brightly up; that the changes of the moon influence the changes of the weather; that even the coincidence of certain phases of the moon with certain days of the week exercises a disastrous influence upon the weather of the ensuing days of the week, or month; that a great profusion of hedge-fruit – 'hips and haws' especially – betokens, not a past favourable fruiting season, but the severity of the coming winter; and so forth.

J.C. Atkinson

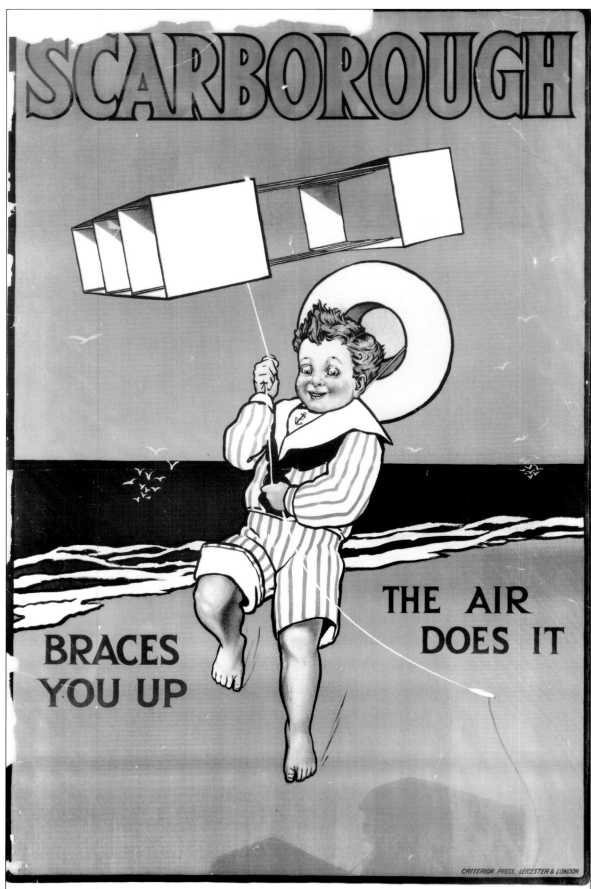

THE *FEARLESS* AT SCARBOROUGH

WILD AND DESOLATE SWALEDALE

The upper Swale between Gunnerside and Keld is the most remote and isolated of Yorkshire dales. The hurry, scurry and press of town life is unknown here – and as if it could not be. No railroad drives its iron horse through or up betwixt these hill barriers that protect it from the delights and risks of modern life. Not yet disturbed or even altered has been the even tenour of the plodding dalesmen's ways. Their occupations, their customs are still in the footsteps of their forefathers. Hemmed within a narrow restricted space, no whistle or boom beyond that of the wintry blast reaches their ears; or the thunderous explosions of a storm in autumn or winter, when clouds roll up over the hills *against* the wind. This highland of Swale is yet a land without its lord, squire or county magistrate. At least not above Gunnerside. It is remote, rural, communal, not unlike those other narrow valleys, of the Swiss cantons; where the race, born simple and natural, died for the most part in the same natural state. Every man holds himself to the simpler tenets of conduct, fearing God, speaking out the truth as they may see it, respecting the rights of others and so guarding their own, albeit holding with sturdiness that all men are equal, with their neighbours. This as in primitive times, for, be it remembered, all are descended

from the sturdy yeomen of old. To-day the dalefolk answer to little more than a score patronymics, of which the Aldersons, Calverts, Clarksons, Closes, Knowles, Fawcetts, Harkers, Keartons, Metcalfs and Scotts are the principal. There has been an immigrant addition (as was to be expected) of one or two quaker families from the neighbour valleys of Eden, 'the West Country,' of Yore, and of Ravenstonedale – Brunskill for instance. Once a fortnight, or less often, a farmer with his wife or daughter will drive to 'the Hawes' by the 'Buttertubs' pass, or to Kirkby Stephen market to sell produce and buy in, the requisite out-world-over-sea necessaries – calico, soap, tea, or what-not.

Those who love wild and desolate scenery will find this remote land a region of strange charm, ever full of new points of interest – simple scenes and simple natures hold reserves and are not fathomed at one interview. The various centres should be visited not only in high summer, when rivers are low and stock care for themselves, but in winter or early spring when every rill is on the 'ring,' and the waters are 'out' of their beds; and again in late autumn. Winter is *later* in its onset and knipe in these deep dales than in the plains of York; the reason is, that the vast hill masses slowly give out back to the air, in November and through December to February, the immense amount of heat which they absorbed through the twenty

CAYTON, NEAR SCARBOROUGH

hour's daylight of June and July: slowly warmed the hills as slowly cool, twining the wheel of the seasons at least a month backward.

Edmund Bogg

VIGNETTE OF GUNNERSIDE

Gunnerside is as yet unaltered, unspoilt, in the primitive beauty that is all its own. The beck bridge, with the village grouped about it, is the hub or pivot of the scene, the gossip ground where the dalesfolk gather and linger makes a complete picture, and one full of light when the sunshine is upon it, as full of awful warning and threat when the skies are 'of lead' with the hills, and the north-wester winds its horn of wail or requiem, or the ruder blasts of Boreas shoot sheets of hail across it. The picture is eloquent too, if one of human kind is, peradventure, in it: a shepherd home-driving his flock of 'yowes' through the street; or an old dalesman leaning heavily on his stick against the wind, after four score years experience of it, here, 'early and late,' as they say (though what would be late for him would be early enough in the towns of the busy plain) in 'Owd Gang'; or, yet again, a lad of sturdy youth astride a rough-coated galloway driving cows to pasture, or a bowed figure with a can of milk strapped upon his shoulders. Such vignettes always give finish and add the touch of human interest to the scene.

Edmund Bogg

ROWDYISM IN THE MOORS

That there may be rowdyism among us still, it would be absurd to dispute; but, at least, it is limited rowdyism, and of a mitigated character. Time was, unquestionably, when such an assertion could not truthfully have been made. But that time had passed before I had ever heard of Danby. But there were men I had a personal acquaintance with soon after I came into residence, who were the last of an expiring class; men whose pastime it had been, if not whose object and desire, to provoke a row or a scuffle, and to fight it out then and there. One of these persons, a stout-built muscular man, even in his old age – he must have been turned of seventy – was described to me as literally the 'hero of a hundred fights.' Poor old William was quiet enough when and after I began to know him; but those who had known him in the elder days said he had, in the days of his strength and vigour, been the most turbulent of a turbulent group. Rows, scuffles, scrimmages had been the rule then, and William, with another still then living, was never out of them. Hardly-contested boxing-bouts, with a cruel amount of 'punishment,' were of continual occurrence, and truly William's scarcely lovely countenance looked as if it had been sorely battered. From all I could hear, the stranger whose devious footsteps brought him to Danby in those old days, was likely to experience something of the 'Heave 'arf a brick at 'im' treatment recorded by George Stephenson as the customary welcome extended by north-country natives to unlucky explorers of the country wilds.

J.C. Atkinson

THE RECTOR LEAVES YARM CHURCH

MOURNERS IN WHITE

Many years ago now, I had been at church on one of these bitterly stormy days which occur from time to time; and I had already been told of a funeral fixed for just after the service. The congregation had barely numbered half a dozen persons all told; and the snow and sleet were driving about on the wings of a fierce wind, so as to make even breathing difficult when one was forced to face it. One of my sons had gone to church with me, a stalwart lad of seventeen or eighteen, and on the conclusion of the service, seeing no signs of the funeral near, he decided not to wait for me but to go home at once. I waited half an hour, and still no signs of the approach of the procession. Another quarter of an hour, and the storm still growing worse every minute. Once and again both I and the clerk had gone out to see, as well as we could, if there was any sign, but without result. At last I began to think something must have interfered with the arrangements, and that we were waiting to no purpose, and I went out to look, for what was to be the last time. It was almost impossible to look out steadily in the direction the funeral was to come, by reason of the stouring snow which blew directly into one's face and eyes; but still I had satisfied myself that there was nothing in

sight; and I had but just decided with the clerk that it was unnecessary to wait any longer. While I was still speaking the chancel (or priest's) door was opened and the figures of two or three men appeared. But they were men in white garments, men of snow in reality. I never saw such figures before. All of them, as usual at a funeral, in black clothes, and yet nothing that was not white with snow about them. They must have been within a hundred yards or so of the churchyard when I had gone for my last look, and yet, from their whitened covering, and the difficulty of looking steadfastly forth against such a storm, I had not been able to descry them. And their story was that they had left Castleton in good time, with the little girl's coffin in the hearse; that the difficulty of getting along the road had been considerable almost from the outset; that after the first half mile it increased with every step, and at last when they had made their way to within three fields of the church, further progress had become impossible for horse or hearse, and they had taken the coffin out to bear it by hand. Then six able-bodied men had taken it – the body was that of a girl under thirteen years of age – and had left the road, and began to struggle across the fields. Before they had made much progress they were of necessity relieved, and other six strong men took up the burden; and alternating in this way, they had

MARKET PLACE, HAWES

at length, and with extreme difficulty and the greatest exertion, achieved the passage of the three fields, or the total distance of less than half a mile.

The service at the grave was a continued physically painful experience. I was compelled to stand with my back to the blast, or it would have been alike impossible to see or to read in such a fierce, savage stour; and the sharp, hard sleet and roughened snow were driven against the unprotected parts of my neck and face with such vehemence and impinged with such force upon the parts already aching with the bitter cold, that no flogging I ever got was in the least to be compared with the smarting experience of those ten minutes.

J.C. Atkinson

A WANDERING SNOWDRIFT

The most extraordinary feat I have ever known as achieved in the way of the making of snowdrifts by our moorland blasts, took place during the winter of 1886–7, and the account of it was given me by the 'gaffer' of the small band of road-minders and menders employed by the township. The wind had blown from the north and east when the snow began to be drivable, and he had had some difficulty in keeping the door of his own dwelling – a house on the very edge of the moor, three-quarters of a mile from the site of my own – and one night he had taken the precaution to carry his shovel indoors, with the almost certainty that he would have to dig his way out in the morning; inasmuch as the passage he had cut and kept clear from day to day was filling fast at the darkening, and there was

every appearance of a terrible night of snow and drifting. Armed with his well-brightened tool – for he had been snow-cutting for days whenever there seemed a chance of doing it to any effect – he opened his door in the early light, and strange, incredible as it seemed, there was no big wreath of snow there – no wreath at all worth thinking of. But at the other end of the house there was a gigantic accumulation piled up, and reaching almost to the gable point of the roof. The wind had shifted during the night and had transported the results of its action during the previous days from the one end to the other! And exactly the same thing had happened at the farmhouse some 200 yards more to the north, and similarly situated.

J.C. Atkinson

SLEDDING ALONG THE WALL TOPS

The vicar of Hardraw has had remarkable experiences during his long ministry in his journeys some six miles or so up to Lunds Church: long detours had to be made, or else balancing walks – acrobatic progressions rather – *along the tops of the walls* for considerable distances! It sounds a 'traveller's tale' of romance to hear accounts of night journeys to outlandish districts by 'parson' or the now venerable medical practitioner of Hawes, who was for years, he and his gig and man Ned, at every ones beck and call. During winters' frosts he discarded wheels and sledded over the wall tops across the hard frozen wind-banked snow.

Edmund Bogg

ON THE SHORE, SCARBOROUGH

THE EVE OF ST AGNES

At midnight on the eve of St. Agnes, a maiden must pluck from the grave of a bachelor a blade of grass, walk backward from the grave to the church gate, and then hurry to her bed-chamber. Safely there, she had to lock her door, hanging the key on a nail outside the window, then undress herself; but – and here comes the difficulty – her various garments had to be removed in the same order as they had been put on, that is, that which she had donned first must be taken off first. This must have been a feat requiring great agility and no little patience, exceeding by a long way the task of skinning an eel in the dark. No doubt everything would be worn very loosely that day, and any undue exertion must have rendered such a maid liable any moment to assume the condition of a statue. Of one thing I am absolutely certain: did the maid accomplish the feat so far as her skirts and other items of her apparel are concerned, she would have to sleep with her boots on, for her stockings would present a problem which jeers at the senile efforts of the Sphinx. But, having performed the said ritual so far, it only remained for her to wrap the blade of grass in a clean sheet of paper, place it under her pillow, leave a burning candle near the window, and retire to rest, when presently she would see the man who was to be her husband open the window, look in, throw the key into the room, close the window, and depart. Where the chamber was on the ground floor, or ladders were handy, I can well understand this ritual would often succeed.

Richard Blakeborough

THE DISAPPEARING ORCHESTRA

Glaisdale has always had an interest in music long before I started. There was a brass band who rehearsed at Mr. Brown's house, The Hall. He had a building with a fireplace in where they practised in winter time, but on fine summer evenings they played in the farmyard. The building I have mentioned was kept specially for the band and was always called the bandhouse. . . .

When I was about eight or nine years old there was an orchestra who practised in the Mechanics' Institute at the bottom of Underhill. This was a mixed orchestra and I remember being at one of their practices, although I was not a member. There were quite a lot of ladies in the orchestra and one played the Double Bass. The trouble with this orchestra was that when they were out playing at Christmas the ladies were often having trouble with their violins, broken strings, etc. In each case a young man would volunteer to help the lady, which they stopped to do while the rest went on. Some of the couples were never seen again that evening and others only caught up with the orchestra when it was time to go home. The orchestra sometimes got so depleted in that way until there were only a few older men and women left to play.

George Harland

31

BOER WAR VETERANS RETURN TO YARM

ON MIDSUMMER'S EVE

There are several charms and ceremonies peculiar to Midsummer Eve, the careful observance of which enables a maiden to learn something of what fate may have in store for her. Does she doubt the constancy of her lover, she can satisfy herself once for all, no matter what other folk may say, and in spite of anything she may have seen or imagined herself, by observing the following rite. Certainly the carrying out of the ceremony is a wee bit troublesome, but of what account is trouble when such vital points are at issue as the unmasking of perfidy or the establishment of truth and love? To perform the rite the maiden must proceed as follows: – Pull three hairs from the tail of a perfectly black cat, also three from a red cow; gather three leaves of the deadly nightshade, and, having killed a white pigeon, smear each leaf with blood from its heart. Now make three flat parcels, each containing a cat's hair, a cow's hair, and a leaf.

Next stew the pigeon, saving the gravy. Now make a savoury dish, adding thereto the gravy. The suspected one must be asked to supper on Midsummer Eve, the damsel being careful to place under the tablecloth the three parcels, in such manner that one will lie under his plate, one under the dish containing the gravy, and the third under her own plate. During supper, should her lover find the least fault with any person or thing, he is faithless. If the maiden is very deeply in love, I should advise her to do most of the talking; let it be only a one-course supper, and hurry through with it. The above charm is rarely resorted to now; the several difficulties which have to be overcome before it can be successfully carried out, have almost laid it on one side. But I well remember its being tried years ago by one of our servants, and I have been informed that it was resorted to, inside the last five years, at a farm-house near Swainby.

Richard Blakeborough

32

CORONATION DAY, WHITBY

'AN ATTRACTION (?) TO WHITBY'

To the Editor of the Whitby Gazette.   31 August 1904

SIR, – Until last Saturday, I was a stranger to Whitby, but I
came then, on strong recommendation from friends, to see
this beautiful old town, and to find rest from a City life. I am
delighted with this place, and the air is all that a jaded city
man could wish; but, unfortunately, I had to arrange my
lodgings by post, and now find myself next door to a steam
roundabout, which is certainly not calculated to do me the
good I expected. I arrived on Saturday, and the music,
principally '*Bill Bailey*', continued until 11.45 p.m. This week
it has continued nightly until ten-thirty. Thinking I might get
some information from the powers that be, as to whether
anything could be done in the matter, I consulted a police
officer. He told me the ground had been let by the Harbour
Board, and nothing could be done to stop the music. I
remarked that evidently there was nothing for me to do but to
shake the dust of Whitby from my feet, and go to a quieter
spot. 'Yes,' he replied, 'perhaps you had better, and so make
room for others.' Of course, if this is the spirit of those who
have the welfare of Whitby at heart, I suppose I, as a stranger,
can say nothing. I enclose my card, and remain, Sir,
Yours truly,

A VISITOR

OLD MARKET PLACE, WHITBY

33

CORONATION CELEBRATIONS, HELMSLEY

THE LAST WOMAN HANGED AT YORK

The barbarian and primitive instincts of those of the moorlanders who had 'bred back' were frequently in evidence. Some of their actions were more than cruel. The dutiful son of one who was eternally 'threeaping' with and 'pashing at' his wife carried out to the letter his father's behest to cut her 'd—d heead off,' decapitated his mother with an axe and on his father's return from market presented him with the head on a charger. The last woman hanged at York was a moorlander. It was the old story of a woman scorned and transformed into a hell-cat. She was thrilled with love for the farmer for whom she kept house, but unfortunately he was not responsive, much preferring, to her deep affection, the excellent fatty 'gaufer' cakes which she made. The stupid man might have endured the former, while revelling in the latter. Having tried in vain all her arts and artfulness, including no doubt spasmodic hysterics, she popped the question only to be refused. The next day during the farmer's absence at market she bought some 'puzzon' (poison) which she mixed with the cakes he so dearly loved. The tipsy old doctor was quite unsuspicious and would have given a certificate of death, had not the significant coincidence of all the farmyard poultry dying after picking up some of the dead man's vomit, been brought to his notice.

R.W.S. Bishop

THE WHITBY BREWSTER SESSIONS

The report of Supt. Pinkney was next read by the Clerk, as follows: –

'To the Justice acting in and for the Petty Sessional Division of Whitby Strand.

Gentlemen, – I have the honour to submit the annual report in reference to the licensed houses in this division.

There are 121 fully licensed houses, one less than last year, namely the Esk Inn, Boghall, demolished October 1903, for railway improvements; nine beer houses, two off-licenses and nine wine licenses, making 141 licenses now in force.

The population of the division is 21,743, giving one licensed house to every 154 inhabitants.

During the year seven innkeepers have been proceeded against, namely, three for permitting drunkenness, one fined £1 and costs, two dismissed; one keeping his house open for the sale of liquor during prohibited hours, to pay costs; one for selling liquor to a child under the age of fourteen years, dismissed; and two for being drunk on their own licensed premises, fined 10s each and costs – one of these persons has since left the house. With these exceptions, so far as is known to the Police, the remainder of the houses have been well-conducted.

Two persons have been proceeded against for being drunk in charge of a child under seven years of age – one fined 2s 6d and 8s 6d costs, and one committed for fourteen days.

TALBOT INN, SCARBOROUGH

The number of persons proceeded against for drunkenness during the year is 110, as compared with eighty-nine in the corresponding period of last year, showing an increase of twenty-one.

I am, gentlemen, Your obedient servant, P. PINKNEY, Superintendent.

Whitby Gazette

THE CAUSES OF INSANITY

The predominating causes [of insanity] appear to be Alcoholic intemperance (to a far less extent, it is pleasant to record, than last year), senile decay and hereditary influence ascertained. While alcoholic abuse undoubtedly is a prominent cause of insanity, directly and indirectly, both in the victim himself and his unfortunate off-spring, it appears to me that its influence has been somewhat exaggerated from confusion of cause and effect. My experience has been that many persons are addicted to the abuse of alcohol *because they are insane*, both moral sense and will-power being undermined already thereby. It is *not* that they become insane, in every instance, because of the previous abuse of alcohol. These latter more often end with a tragic suddenness from Pneumonia, Cerebral hoemorrhage, &c., and do not live long enough for chronic alcoholism to undermine their mental stability. Alcohol certainly causes some of the acuter insanities; but these, being little more than aggravated *delirium tremens*, appear to be some of our most hopeful cases for recovery. Among other causes the following may be noted: – Three women were admitted suffering from self-accusatory Melancholia, of these two were remorse-stricken because they had attempted medicinal abortion (fortunately without success) – in one case there turned out to be no pregnancy which, when demonstrated, removed the burden on her mind; in the other case she was delivered of a healthy child in due course, and though she declared the drug taken had injured one of its feet, she ultimately overcame this fancy and recovered. In the third case abortion had apparently been performed for Medical reasons, and the shock and remorse of the supposed 'unpardonable sin' unhinged her. She also made a good recovery. A similar self-accusatory condition was found in the case of a woman admitted through intense remorse after adultery. She also got over it.

Middlesbrough Mental Hospital Report, 1901

THE FARMERS ARMS INN, SCORTON

'WHERE THE H— HAVE I BEEN FOR T'LAST WEEK'

Years ago I used to spend a lot of time with Jim on the Hambleton Hills, where we used to take him before the August meetings to keep him away from drink and get him fit to ride at Redcar, Stockton, York and Doncaster.

We used to go rabbiting with dogs and ferrets and took long walks together, and he often said during the course of our rambles that he'd give £5,000 if he had a will strong enough to keep away from drink. I have ridden in many races with him and can tell you he was a great jockey when he was sober and fit, and almost as good as any we have now when he was drunk. He once went to Chester to ride for the Duke of Westminster, and when he arrived at the hotel at which he always stayed, he remarked to the landlord: 'Things are very quiet for the races to-morrow. Has no one turned up yet?'

'Races!' replied the landlord; '*they were last week*, and everyone was asking "Where's Jim Snowden?"'

'Last week, were they?' reiterated Snowden. '*Then where the H— have I been for t' last week?*'

Of course he'd had one of his periodical outbursts of drinking and had forgotten all about Chester races and his mounts there for his grace. He never rode for the Duke of Westminster again after that.

J. Fairfax-Blakeborough

FAIR SHARES IN BED

Nearly all the tales of Yorkshiremen turn upon his wonderful ability to take care of himself. A Yorkshireman arrived one night at an inn, and found every bed engaged. As it was a wet night, one of the company took pity on him, and offered to let the new-comer share his bed. When bed time came, the owner of the room politely asked the Yorkshireman if he preferred to lie on the right or on the left side. To this came the startling rejoinder: 'You can lie which side you like, but I intend to lie in the middle!'

Revd A.N. Cooper

A CUNNING BARGAIN

On the stage we are all familiar with the jolly, hearty friend up from Yorkshire, but no one should suppose he is all sugar, and can be easily gulped down. I knew of a man who had a small piece of land in the midst of a great landlord's estate. The big man wanted to get it at any price, and offered to cover it with sovereigns. To this the owner agreed, but when the agents came, prepared to fulfil the bargain, and laid the money flat on the floor, the owner said, 'Nay! I meant the sovereigns to be placed *edgeways!*'

Revd A.N. Cooper

THE POST OFFICE, TERRINGTON

LAST POST AT RUNSWICK

The steep paths and flights of roughly-built steps that wind above and below the cottages are the only means of getting about in Runswick. The butcher's cart every Saturday penetrates into the centre of the village by the rough track which is all that is left of the good firm road from Hinderwell after it has climbed down the cliff. To this central position, close to the post-box, the householders come to buy their supply of meat for Sunday, having their purchases weighed on scales placed on the flap at the back of the cart. While the butcher is doing his thriving trade the postman arrives to collect letters from the pillar-box. Placing a small horn to his lips, he blows a blast to warn the villagers that the post is going, and, having waited for the last letter, climbs slowly up the steep pathway to Hinderwell.

Halfway up to the top he pauses and looks over the fruit-trees and the tiles and chimney-pots below him, to the bright blue waters of the bay, with Kettleness beyond, now all pink and red in the golden light of late afternoon. This scene is more suggestive of the Mediterranean than Yorkshire, for the blueness of the sea seems almost unnatural, and the golden greens of the pretty little gardens among the houses seem perhaps a trifle theatrical; but the fisher-folk play their parts too well, and there is nothing make-believe about the

WILLIAM RAINE, POSTMASTER, WEST AYTON

MAYNARD'S BRIDGE, SWAINBY

delicious bread-and-butter and the newly-baked cakes which accompany the tea awaiting us in a spotlessly clean cottage close by.

Gordon Home

COUNTRY CURIOSITY

My neighbours perhaps differed more from one another in character, personality, and habits than human beings ordinarily do. Such differences were conspicuous in a sparsely populated country, and became exaggerated by isolation.

Dwellers in towns, like stones in the pot-hole of a river-bed, have all their edges and peculiarities rounded off.

In the country, on the other hand, there is so much elbow-room for everybody that individual eccentricities are accentuated, and the edges of character become sharp and rugged. Moreover, in the country, everybody knows everything about everybody and seeks to know more.

Curiosity is rampant. It is said that country people will even look down the chimney to see what their neighbours are having for breakfast. An unused chimney sending forth for the nonce its volume of smoke advertises to the country-side that something unusual is on foot. 'Another chimbley smoking at Trotter's this morn.' 'What's up? Onnyways t'bairn isn't looked for yet awhile. Must be his sister fra Lunnon, or yon painting chap is there ageean.' Country curiosity is insatiable. Paul Prys abound. Eavesdropping is no disgrace. One salutes the passer-by in the dark, purely in order to recognise the voice and guess what his business may be. The village postman in those days would read all the correspondence he could, and then retail it for his neighbours' benefit. One local postman I knew made a sad blunder. After steaming two letters open he put the letters into the wrong envelopes, and of course there was trouble, which sent him back to cobbling and bitter reflections.

R.W.S. Bishop

38

FISHING FLEET, SCARBOROUGH

A Night Sketch at Hawes

After tea a pipe of 'bacca and a stroll through the town. A group of men stand in the market place; the non-believers are arguing with the Christians; the shoemaker is holding forth, anon they all speak together, each side quotes from divers learned books, whereat Bob Routh calls loudly for chapter and verse, 'gie us th' chapter an' verse.' For such a small town there is quite a surprising number of non-believers; and erstwhile the low sinking sun is reddening the hill tops, and while the carillon in the church tower is playing its quaint sweet evening hymn, they argue and squabble over their different dogmas. Let us leave them and have a chat with the ancient men on the bridge, meditating, as usual. Slowly they turn themselves round, leisurely they take their clay pipes from their mouths, knowingly they look up and observe the signs of the sky; at last they speak, 'aye, it leuks like bein' middlin' weather to-morn, aye,' whereat they thrust their pipes if possible farther in their mouths than before, and resume their silent watching. We pass on. The twilight wanes, the phosphorescence on the western hills dies away, and now the moon appears over the black edge of Wether Fell. Yawber and the long sharp wall of limestone at its top stand out clear and black; the rest is in deep shadow. Evidently the opinion of the 'owd 'uns' is going to be confirmed. Now they are gone and the bridge is deserted. Not so the market place, the theologists are bickering yet; if it were not moonlight, they would, no doubt, have a lantern, they often do. But now for a last pipe and a drop of 'hot,' and so to bed, lulled to slumber by the rushing sound of Gayle beck, hurrying past the walls of our bedroom.

Edmund Bogg

'The Angel of the Inn'

Yet another figure of pathetic interest was that of Sarah (the Angel of the Inn), whose mental vision, sad to say, had become wholly impaired. A pitiful sight, indeed, giving pause to all levity from the forceful way in which it pointed the human and divine connexion linking body to soul. The beauteous habitation was there without its holy tenant. Her wondrously striking 'raven's-wing' locks, her glossy and long black hair, her darkly liquid almost luminous eyes, without the vital spark of understanding, contrasted with a face whose skin was of ivory delicacy, made up a picture of sweet, too sweet, docility over which one might fancy a fairy angel typifying Womanhood weeping, since naught but an infinite pity might be felt for the fair blighted bud. On our first visit – and indeed at subsequent ones – we were strangely impressed by that 'vacant chair' of feminity. It was night when we entered the old inn, where the huge banked-up fire allowed deep Rembrandtish shadows to be cast by intervening furniture, and we were barely seated before our attention was rivetted by poor Sarah sitting idly, hands on lap, in meekest pose. She appeared to live in a beautiful spiritual world of which we common mortals could have no conception. Then, suddenly, yet without violence, she would seem to arouse herself from reverie, and commence weaving with her hands and a graceful curve of arms a skein of wondrous imaginary threads: such a pose and play in dumb show as not even the greatest of actors could emulate, such delicacy and grace of movement was there! The ethereal loveliness of the poor girl's face, her shining lights of eyes that yet shot forth no message beam, her intricate waving of hands, has not even yet been erased from the writer's memory, though difficult to convey in words.

Edmund Bogg

DANBY LODGE

END OF THE WORLD AT DANBY

Another event happened at Danby Head sometime after we had left there. There was at that time a great controversy in the newspapers about a man who had prophesied the end of the world. The newspapers made a lot of this many weeks before the event was supposed to take place. At Danby Head there was a little holding called St. Helena. From this place there is a good view of the head of Danby dale. The man who farmed this holding turned out early one morning, which happened to be the very morning of the so called end of the world, and there before his eyes it was breaking up. The sheep were running and the trees were leaning over at acute angles then righting themselves and leaning over in the opposite direction. The ground was all rolling and twisting and was all on the move. The farmer did not run away as he thought one place was as good as another at the end of the world. However, he lived to realise that it was a huge landslide which can still be seen as you pass up Castleton Rigg.

George Harland

BUILDING DANBY HALL

After finishing the house at Goathland five of us were sent to Danby Head to start to build the new hall there for a man called G.A. MacMillan a London Publisher. After walking up the dale to the proposed site a distance of four miles, we arrived in the field where the building was to be situated and found four little white pegs driven into the ground to mark the place where this building to be called Botton Hall was to be built. We found lodgings near to the site, where were boarded from Monday till Saturday. For this we paid ten shillings per week, and were well fed and made very comfortable. This was in the year 1899. . . .

To pass the time at our lodgings in the long winter evenings, there were many activities, one was card playing another fret saw work. There was an ambulance class for first aid and the Macmillans supplied us with plenty of books to read. . . .

I with two other youths worked in a shed alongside four stonemasons, making seven bankers (benches) in that shed. I remember dressing my first chamfered four foot mullion. A lot of care was needed as these mullions were very slender. I was a very proud youth indeed when the kind old man who worked on the next bench to me and who had shown me how to do it, called up the older masons to my banker. He took a straight edge and tested my stone for them to see. He was as proud as I was of my work. I hope I may be excused for mentioning this.

George Harland

'SOMEWHAT PRIMITIVE PEOPLE' OF SWALEDALE

The mountain streams in this part of the dale have their charms for the angler, and the moors for the sportsman, while both moor and stream afford pleasure to those who love nature in her wildness and solitude. But only they who can endure fatigue, and philosophically content themselves with such accommodation as the somewhat primitive people can afford, should undertake to explore this remote part of Upper Swaledale.

Black's Picturesque Guide to Yorkshire, 1882

MOWING BRACKEN, FARNDALE

HAWES IN HAYING-TIME

It is well to visit Hawes in the haying-time, and inhale deep breaths of the perfume of newly-mown half dry grass off the sweet limestone meads, and store it up in your memory when in less rural scenes; or if you are a fly-fisher come up to Hawes in Spring, when the primroses dapple the ground of the water side copses with clots of bloom, and go a-fishing for the speckled trout or the sleek silver grayling along with 'Sproats' – the 'watcher' of these waters! His skill has something of the uncanny in it – he can hook a trout, or more, at one cast where others fail, and the meanwhile reel you many a yarn.

Edmund Bogg

SHEEP WASHING DAYS

Sheep had to be washed every year before their wool could be sold to the wool buyers. Special folds were built in small streams for this purpose, many of which can still be seen today, but in a lot of cases the stone has been carted away to be used for other purposes.

Sometimes the water was dammed up to the required height and a barrel was placed in the middle of it. A man would stand in the barrel so that he could keep dry and the sheep were passed to him and he would dip them and turn them out at the other side. In some cases the farmers would join together and take the sheep down to the river Esk near to Beggars Bridge where there was a large fold which could hold two or three hundred sheep at a time. A man was appointed to get into the river in old clothes, opposite the sheep fold. He would stand in the water up to his hips. Another man would stand by the side of the stream and take the sheep from the boys who were catching them and he would throw the sheep one at a time of course to the man in the stream who would wash them and turn them out of the stream at the opposite side. These were great days for the boys of the village and as there was always a gallon of beer on the site many a boy had his first taste of beer at a sheep washing. There is a good picture of this sheepwash at Beggars Bridge amongst Mr. Frank Sutcliffe's pictures.

George Harland

THATCHED HAYSTACKS, SKIPLAY GRANGE

SHEEPDOGS FIERCE AS WOLVES

I think I knew every sheep-dog in the country, and from long experience affirm very decidedly that no sheep-dog can be trusted to make friends with one. An unfriendly, fierce and brave sheep-dog is an ugly customer to tackle, but when it came to two of them I was obliged to get my back to a stone wall and keep them off as well as I could with the stout stick I always carried, until help came. I remember walking across the moorland with a friend, when we were attacked by two savage dogs, which I knew quite well. They saw us a long way off and flew towards us. We had to get back to back till we got up to the shelter of a stone wall, where they kept us till the farmer came to our assistance. They were as fierce as wolves and made terrific leaps in the air. It is the blow on the front legs you must try and get home if possible. The old stone-throwing dodge only infuriates them.

R.W.S. Bishop

THE MAGPIE

One for sorrow, two for luck,
Three for a wedding, four for a death,
Five for silver, six for gold,
Seven for a bonny lass twenty years old.

Richmond Chronicle, 1907

ORIGINAL POETRY ON THE YEAR OF OUR LORD, 1895

When April came it was so fine
All through the month the sun did shine;
And then it came such splendid showers,
On every side sprung up the flowers;
The birds they then began to sing,
The cuckoo did good tidings bring;
The rook he crew though he was so dark,
And then went towering up the lark;
The farmer rose before 'twas light,
And worked with might from morn till night,
And then retired to his rest
Content that he had done his best;
When morning came he was up again,
Away he went to sow his grain,
And when the soil was clear of weed,
To sow good seed he did take heed.

The next that came was the Month of May,
It rained and blew from day to day,
And some who thought their labour lost,
Before it went out there was such a frost.

The month of June it was so dull
We thought the wheat would never be full,
And barley too as well as oats
Would both be troubled alike with shorts.

John Magginson

THE NOTED CHOCOLATE STORES, FORGE VALLEY

A FRIGHTENING GRANDFATHER

As a very young child, I was mortally afraid of my grandfather. Yet the one time I had anything to do with him then, he behaved with great gentleness. My mother had been thrashing me. Made reckless by my fear of pain, I ran wildly round my bedroom, howling, trying to dodge the cane. Exhausted, she told me, 'I must bring your grandfather to deal with you.'

She left the house and I waited, in the state of self-induced apathy, a sort of stupor made up of dislike of showing distress, fear of being pitied, and a purely instinctive animal immobility, in which – so far – I have always been able to sink myself at will. Crouched on the landing outside my room, I watched my grandfather between the balusters as he came up the last flight; he halted half way up, stared at me for a moment and, to my great astonishment, said only, 'You shouldn't wear your mother out,' then turned and went down.

In those days it was the custom to thrash children. Few people imagined that they could be trained by any methods except those used on savagely unbroken horses. Whitby may have been backward in this respect (as in some others), still early Victorian, but not, I think, a great deal. My mother herself was impatient, easily bored, and perhaps more determined to bring her children up well than were some few of her contemporaries.

The cruelty of the method lay in its deliberateness. *I shall thrash you when we get home* had the ring of a death sentence. Any act of carelessness or disobedience outside the house merited it. If other people were present, the offender might get only a terrible glance, a warning what to expect. The pupil of my mother's eye seemed to send out a flash of light, like the discharge from a gun: I have never seen another such glance. The walk home might be short or long; no delay was long enough to ward off the assault of bared flesh and stretched nerves. And the business of forgiveness, which came hours later, was as emotionally racking as the punishment itself.

Only at this moment, as I write, sixty years after the event, I realize that when my grandfather halted and looked up, he saw a desperate little animal behind bars.

Storm Jameson

AN ILLEGITIMATE GRANDMOTHER

My *real* grandfather, my mother's *real* father, became biggest horse dealer in the north of England. And when it came Askrigg Hill Fair, he always used to come to Hill Top and have his lunch with us. But me mother never liked him

OLD COTTAGE AND BECK, HELMSLEY

coming, because she never got over being illegitimate, you know. So she was always in a bad temper when he came, and one time she snapped at him about something: and I'll always remember how he walked up to her and put his hand on her shoulder, and he said; 'Belle, I always owned you were mine, and you *are* mine: and I've never run off it.' But me mother, she didn't want to know, and she'd never be friends with him. Us kiddies thought he was grandest fella living, though, because he always gave us a shilling each!

He never *had* run off it, mind. He would have married me granny, but she wouldn't have him, no. In them days lads like him had no money, you know: they worked at home, and they didn't get a wage, they never got a penny. So he had no money to marry with, and *daren't* tell what he'd done, at first. Because Grandmother was a servant girl in the house, you see, and *he* was the son of the family: and it was a big let down for the son to marry the servant girl, in them days. But when it did come up, his two old aunties that lived here with him said, 'You'll get her married!' And he says, 'I can't marry her, I've nae money.' So they gave him a hundred pound (which was a lot of money in them days) and set him off walking over to Muker to marry me granny. But *she* wouldn't have him. Because by then she'd got stout with me mother, and she says, '*I'm* not going into no church a disgrace!' She never did have him: and afterwards he went over to Reeth, and started taking horses to fairs, and he became biggest horse dealer in north of England. Woodward was his name.

Maggie Joe Chapman

FAMILY PORTRAIT, MIDDLESBROUGH

THE DEMAINE SISTERS, KEARTON

REMEDIES FOR WHOOPING COUGH

. . . only the other day I was told that if a field-mouse was skinned and made into a small pie and eaten, and the warm skin bound hair-side against the throat, and kept there for nine days, the worst whooping cough ''at ivver was' would be cured.

Speaking of whooping cough, I remember a lady at Guisborough, only a few years ago, taking both her boys to the gasworks for them to inhale the fumes from the gas-tank. It nearly poisoned the whole three, but the cough survived it nicely. However, that and the field-mouse were infinitely preferable to the recipe I had from an old dame, who assured me 'no cough o' no kind whatsoever could stan' agaan it.' It was this: equal quantities of hare's dung and owl's pellets – the latter are the disgorged remains of feathers, bones, &c., which the owl objects to digest. Well, having carefully mixed these two ingredients with dill-water, clay, and the blood of a white duck, the resulting filth had to be made into pills the size of a nut, three of which had to be taken fasting on going to bed. This was to be continued until the cough was cured or the patient buried. A much simpler method is to catch a frog, open its mouth and cough into it three times, throw the poor brute over your left shoulder, and the patient will be cured at once. If not, depend upon it there is some very good reason why the charm has failed. One woman I knew, used to take her little girl and hold her over an old well when a bad fit of coughing seized the child. She declared, if at the time either a frog or a toad happened to be at the bottom of the well with its mouth open, the child would be cured instantly. I offered to catch her a frog and open its mouth for the child to cough into; this she objected to, because, as she said, the frog might spit at it and injure it for life. This belief in the poisonous and spitting power of frogs is still retained by the good people of Great Ayton, and also of many other places. . . .

Still another plan may be tried to ease the little sufferers. If they be passed nine times under the belly and over the back of either a piebald pony or an ass (the latter preferred), the cough will be immediately charmed away, whilst a touch on the larynx from the hand of a seventh son of a seventh son is held to be a certain cure. And a hairy caterpillar or small wood-lizard tied round the child's neck, having been stitched in a small bag, was, and I believe is yet, looked upon as a sovereign remedy.

Richard Blakeborough

STEPPING STONES AT HUTTON-LE-HOLE

A 'SWEET' HOLIDAY

FRIDAY. – Our last day on the moors dawned on us with a bright sky and fresh westerly breeze; our luggage had preceded us on the Thursday, so no cares on that score.

We are now looking forward with much pleasure to revisiting our old, favourite haunts at Rievaulx and Helmsley. Another fortnight to be spent in the enjoyment of more of nature's pictures, not less pleasurable because so well known. Our only drawback is our drive to Kirby Moorside; unfortunately, an exchange from the steady, sure-footed horse, so well suited to the rough roads, had been made in favour of a handsomer quadruped, *fresh* from the fields, which had a most disagreeable propensity of taking fright at the most innocent things; its last aversion being to a very quiet, aged, white donkey; this it so resolutely shrunk from, that we were nearly landed in the ditch; it was not with much regret we bid good-bye to this creature.

We had to wait at the King's Head, for the bus which was to take us to Helmsley. As our first day at Kirby Moorside closed with rain, so it seemed to accompany us thither, and, ere we had finished our repast, it came rolling down the street in a rapid stream. For two hours we were prisoners, yet, thankful for shelter, and still more so, as we knew our journey to Helmsley would be in a covered conveyance. The rain had not ceased when we found ourselves comfortably seated in the bus; the other occupants were two young country women and a wee prattling girl, of about two or three years old, whose restless excitement was only held in check by barley sugar, peppermint, and other drops; mother and auntie apparently enjoying the sweetmeats as much as the child. They looked incredulous at a gentle hint that so many sweets were not good for the little one, (and we could have said for themselves also, as we had each observed, how the lack of attention to the teeth had spoilt two nice looking faces). It was evidently a holiday, and they were intent on making it a *sweet* one.

Two Sunday School Teachers

TANNERY WORKERS, AISLABY

'BOILED BOOT SHOPS'

The question of boots, both for children and grown-up people, is with the badly-off a constant difficulty, and one of the most serious that they have to face; and the miserable foot-gear of the women and children especially — the men are obliged to have more or less good boots to go to work in — is a constant source of discomfort and of injury to health. One reason why so many of the poor women go about with skirts which drag about in the mud is that they do not want to display what they have on their feet by holding their skirts up. A working-girl said on one occasion that she thought the mark of a 'real lady' was that she wore a short skirt and neat boots, this last representing to the working-girl almost the unattainable. Boiled-boot shops are still met with. 'Boiled' boots are old boots begged, found in the street, etc., picked up, patched, polished and sold at a low price. There are various old-clothes shops, market stalls, hawkers barrows, at which men's suits as well as women's clothes can be bought for a trifling sum.

Lady Bell

CLOGS FROM GUNNERSIDE

. . . then, a lot of people used to wear clogs: there was a proper clogger in every village. We used to get ours from Gunnerside, from old Batty's, they called him: and he'd repair wir clogs as well. If they wanted new woods [soles] on, Mother used to send us off to Gunnerside with wir clogs on, and he did 'em while we were there. He'd keep us all day, but he was a wonderful fella, because he'd talk away to us, and of course, he always got all t'news of Hill Top off us — and he always gave us a meal. Oh aye, *he* used to give us a meal. But when horses was to shoe, we had to take them to the Gunnerside snith — he was a Calvert. Now he used to keep us all day, too, but he nivver gave us anything: he'd shut up shop for *his* dinner, but he never gave us anything at all.

So our clogs came from old Batty, and our knickers and that we had from Gill the grocer, that used to come once a month from Askrigg. He used to go round all the farms. He came at Monday, with his bag on his back, full of vests and knickers and underwear, and he took his orders then for his groceries — a stone of sugar and all that sort o' thing: and then his cart came at Wednesday, wi' t'stuff on.

Maggie Joe Chapman

47

MIDDLESBROUGH

THE BACK STREETS OF MIDDLESBROUGH

At the present time in Middlesbrough back streets not less than 12 feet wide are constructed for secondary means of access to the back of the houses. In the older portion of the borough narrow back passages, in some cases only 3 feet wide, have been permitted. These, aggravated by privy closets abutting thereon, are, it must be admitted, very detrimental to the sanitary welfare of the surroundings. Back streets are not necessary having regard to the fact that w.c.'s are compulsory for all houses and premises that are now erected.

The erection of privy closets is now a thing of the past. Since July, 1909, it has not been permissible to build houses with privies. Every house is provided, in the case of small houses, with one outside w.c., and the larger houses one w.c. outside and at least one inside. Day work for house refuse collection is now in part carried out. Night scavenging for the emptying of privies, when the conversion of the privy system into w.c.'s is finally carried out, will not be necessary. The Corporation have now in hand the work of conversion of the whole of the existing privy middens into w.c.'s at an estimated cost of £12,000, of which the Corporation pay half. In addition we are also carrying out the conversion of the ordinary privies into w.c.'s for sanitary improvement on another clustered area, and it is hoped that in due course the whole of the privies in Middlesbrough will be done away with and w.c.'s substituted.

S.E. Burgess

BUDGET NO. 4

The family consists of a father, aged 25, mother 25, and three children all under 4. The father is a labourer and works irregularly, as he often complains of being ill. During the thirteen weeks this budget was being kept the mother earned, on the average, about 2s. 6d. per week. All the children look ill and rickety, and are very small and poorly developed, the two youngest being unable to walk. They possess little vitality. Mr. and Mrs. S. live in a house with four rooms, which faces east, and gets little sun, as it is situated in a narrow passage with a high wall on the opposite side. The living room contains comfortable furniture; there are lace curtains in the window, and many ornaments adorn the walls. The rent of the house is 3s. 10½d. weekly, the rates being paid by the landlord. Mrs. S. is tidy in person, and the house and children are spotlessly clean. The food is bought in small quantities. Mrs. S. buys hot suppers sometimes or fried fish and potatoes, or sausages and potatoes. The children eat little at meal times, but have sweet biscuits given them between meals. The family is heavily in debt. The protein in this family's diet only amounts to one-half of the standard requirements, and the total energy value shows a deficiency of 27 per cent.

B. Seebohm Rowntree

48

SWAINBY BRASS BAND

A STREET SCENE IN YORK

Anyone observing a certain little party of shoppers in the city of York on a particular day in the eighteen-eighties might have seen a flashy young woman with a bold expression on her face, easily flushing cheeks, large sentimental blue eyes and a mouth of voluptuous lips, in charge of three miserable-looking, badly dressed little girls, with pig-tails hanging down their backs.

These were the three little Parker girls, of whom I was the middle one. Sometimes on visiting the shops, the governess would peremptorily order us to remain outside, which was certainly what I preferred, as I disliked shops and shopping and yet found that the bustle of the city excited my interest.

I used to 'stand like a stuffed pig' watching carts and carriages, and dogs picking their way in and out of the traffic, and errand boys carrying baskets, and roadmen cleaning the gutters. Especially the latter. There was a road-scraper in constant use upon the roads (for it was long before the day of macadamized surfaces), which fascinated us as we watched it being put into use. It was a sharp scraper, about the width of a wheelbarrow, mounted like an outsize razor on a wooden frame propelled by two wheels.

An iron bar across the front protected the user from the actual scraper and served as a handle wherewith he could either pull or push the vehicle.

He would cross the road and scrape mud and stones to the gutter, making a return journey over the next width that required his services. A cart came along later to receive by dint of shovel and broom all the collection in both gutters, and it was a pleasure to us to notice how little was lost of the semi-liquid mud.

Another feature of the York streets was the Coney Street band, which consisted of three men playing respectively a harp, a cornet and a trombone. They were very popular and reaped a good pecuniary harvest. The cornet player inspired us with a desire to go and do likewise, and we went so far as to approach a man in the music shop and enquire from him as to how we could learn and who could teach us. But the answer was discouraging.

'I could teach you,' he said. 'But I shouldn't think of doing so. Any of those kinds of instruments would blow all your front teeth out. . . .'

So, wisely, we thought again.

Ethel, Lady Thomson

BIRD'S EGG COLLECTORS, RAVENSCAR

'BEACH-WATCHERS'

. . . among sea-side people there are a few who describe their trade as that of beach-watchers, and make a living at it too. The beach-watcher is all day on the shore, and with a gun in his hand will now and again get a wild goose, or some sand grouse, and occasionally may kill a bird rare enough to bring good payment from a naturalist. Then there is at times a crown paid by the coroner for finding a dead body, and insignificant flotsam and jetsam which the coast-guard won't trouble about, such as wood and cordage is constantly picked up. The beach-watcher knows where the birds build their nests and the foxes make their holes, and as nobody could hunt foxes on the beach, he takes license to shoot them, they fetch half a sovereign a-piece; and an ornithologist sometimes pays well to be shown the 'courts' where the rock-dove lays its eggs. In the intervals of business, the beach-watcher amuses himself as best he can.

Bob Cammish was a beach-watcher, and one day when the tide was exceptionally low, he was able to get farther out on the rocks than ever he had been before, and there he descried an opening in the cliffs which he felt it his duty to investigate. The passage was a low one, but Bob was small, and he crept on and upwards until he knew it was time to return, or the tide would cut him off.

Next day he took with him a comrade, and together they entered the hole, and crept further than Bob had been before,

and then the foul air, which is the crux of all those underground passages, began to overpower them, and they had to return to the opening to breathe. Sea-faring men are generally charged with plenty of strong tobacco, which is the best safeguard in foul drains and the like, and so they filled their pipes and tried again. They found their way blocked by some wooden obstruction, which turned out to be a barrel. Barrels are meant to be broached, and a beacher-watcher always had some rough tools about him, so with these Bob discovered the contents of the cask to be brandy. The couple sampled its contents wisely, and not too well, so they were able to get safely home, and kept the knowledge of their prize to themselves. But how could the secret be kept? How could a poor man be possessed of an unlimited store of brandy, and how could that expensive spirit be sold in ginger beer bottles and jugs at a quarter of its usual price without someone 'smelling a rat'? So the coast-guard got wind of it, Bob confessed to the secret of his hidden brandy, and next low tide the Revenue Officers organised a raid upon the underground passage. They took Bob with them, and reached the barrel, but only to find it empty. . . .

So it would seem that while officials had been planning and talking, someone else had been more alert, and had drawn off the entire contents of the barrel, which was said to have been sold to a Scarborough publican.

Revd A.N. Cooper

MARKET DAY, NORTHALLERTON

A LONELY DEATH

I shall never forget the deep impression made on my mind by the case of a certain sheep farmer, who was dying by inches from a painful cancer. He had never married, and his only companion, his housekeeper, was a grim, silent old woman, with apparently not a particle of human love or sympathy in her composition. He never read, and there he lay in that lonely and remote farmhouse, always in discomfort or pain, with no one to love, to be loved by, for nearly two long years, waiting without a murmur and with most stoical resignation for the order of release. Such a picture of a lonely heart touches the depth of human pathos. In old age love is as necessary as in childhood.

R.W.S. Bishop

THE BOTTLE-CORK SELLER

The writer can remember how old people — natives of the dales — could relate how a neighbour's sheepdog found, after a severe snowstorm, the decaying body of this or that old man, who had perished in the snow at Wintergill; or the finding of an old man's bleached bones near to Bluewath Beck, not far from an ancient sheepfold, where sheep were washed in the hot days of summer.

This old man used to travel these moor roads from one place to another selling bottle corks, which he disposed of to the farmers' wives, and his chief customers, the wayside innkeepers. Often he would call at Hamer, where he was usually sure of a small business transaction with the writer's mother, which is how the writer came to know of him. His skeleton body was identified by the scattered bottle corks lying nearby, and the basket in which he carried them, which was beginning to decay. It is just possible he was on his way to make this small transaction — as Hamer was not far away — when the snowstorm overtook him.

Joseph Ford

FIREMAN AND WINDOW REPAIRER

We youngsters used to look forward eagerly in the Spring and Summer to the evenings . . . when the Fire Brigade came out for a 'wet' practice, their cart loaded with reels or hose and other fire-fighting gear, and helped or hindered considerably during the itinerary by a horde of mischievous children. The main practice seemed to consist of connecting the hydrant, quickly (at first) running out the hose and training the jets of water on to the walls and windows of the various hostelries, giving them a good wash

MARKET PLACE, PICKERING

down. Inevitably, and properly, the landlord 'washed down' the firefighters and then they would proceed to the next, repeating this aquatic process until in due course, the eleven pubs were shining bright – and so were many of the firemen. Long before the exercise was completed most of the brigade were nice and damp inside and outside, and the young supporters thoroughly soaked. By Thursday, it was not uncommon to be hard up, so you see it was a good, well chosen time to have the practice. . . .

Old 'Rattler,' a hardy member of the Brigade, among many other things did a spot of property repairing including glazing. It was said that on arriving at the scene of a fire, he lost no time in putting his axe through a window or two. Next day, if all went well, he was repairing windows.

Maurice E. Wilson

A VANISHED INDUSTRY

The third vanished industry of the Riding is jet digging, the refuse heaps of which are studded at intervals, at a uniform level, along the face of the *Cleveland* hills behind Stokesley and on the slopes of *Bilsdale* and *Scugdale*. The rain of centuries will not wash them away, and vegetation refuses to hide them.

But the digging has ceased; and though the carving of jet is still carried on at *Whitby*, the jet itself is foreign.

Joseph E. Morris

'MOOR POUT'S' PERSONAL CLOCK

I one day asked a moorsider, or a 'moor pout', as these people call themselves, hurrying along the moorland road, how his wife and daughter, whom I was attending, were. Without troubling to stop, he kept on at the same pace answering my questions over his shoulder in what I thought a very rude and surly fashion. A few days later I tackled him about it. His explanation was very simple. He was sexton of the moorland church, and it was his task to keep the clock in order. But he had no watch. He used to walk the eight miles over the moors to the moorland town every week to make his family purchases, and, when ready to return, would note the correct time of day by the post-office clock. From long experience he knew almost to a minute how long it would take him, going at a fixed pace, to reach home. The clocks of the dale were then set by this scientific and accurate method. They were notoriously correct.

R.W.S. Bishop

WEDDING AT BATTERSBY JUNCTION

THE 'AWKWERD JOB' OF MARRYING

Three farms on the south side of the Swale opposite Muker, go by the singular name of Rash – in other parts of the country the term Rash connotes a young wood or new plantation. At one of these steadings dwelt a family named Alderson, the mother there living to a good old age: in fact her two sons had passed middle age themselves, and neither had married. When the mother died, in course of years the bachelor couple found themselves in somewhat of a dilemma as regards the domestic drudgery that usually falls to the female on a farm. The younger said to the elder, 'John, thoo mun wed' – the retort being, 'Nay, nay, *thoo* mun wed!' This shuttlecock sort of argument was kept up for some considerable time, but at length John the elder gave way, remarking, 'Ay, if ivver there wor an awkwerd job, I allus get it,' and so took upon his shoulders the burden of that contract the term of which is comprised in 'till death do us part.'

Edmund Bogg

A POCKETFUL OF MONEY

The almost invariable practice on the part of the newly married man has been, and still is, after the registration in the vestry has been duly attended to, and when the party are just on the point of leaving the church, to hand to the officiating minister, nominally in payment of the fees, a handful, sometimes a very large handful, of money, taken without the slightest pretence of counting it from his trousers pocket, from which the said minister is expected to take the usual fees for parson and clerk; and, that done, to hand over the surplus to the bride. Twice within my incumbency a deviation from this ritual – and a very pretty deviation – has occurred. The bridegroom, together with the ring, at the proper point in the service, has laid upon the book the aforesaid handful of money, so that, besides the direct pertinency of the next following part of the service, viz. 'With this ring I thee wed,' ensued a typification of the further sentence, 'With all my worldly goods I thee endow.'

J.C. Atkinson

THE BRIDE-WAIN

As to what the bride-wain really was. When I first came into residence here, there were few farmhouses in which there was not one of those fine old black oak cabinets or 'wardrobes,' with

53

CHURCH PARADE, WEST AYTON

carved panels, folding-doors, and knobby feet, that have gladdened so many collectors' hearts; in not a few cases I have seen them in old cottages also. And not once or twice only, but many times I have heard the name 'bride-wain' attributed to them. The word itself was sufficient to suggest if not to provoke inquiry. For the 'wain' was a vehicle that went upon wheels, and upon two wheels rather than four; because the wain upon four wheels speedily became a waggon, and ceased to be a wain. But a press or wardrobe certainly is not a vehicle, however much it may be a repository.

But the wardrobe might be, and often was in the olden times, a constituent portion of the 'wedding presents,' which always partook of the homely and useful character, almost to the exclusion of the merely graceful or pretty, and much more the sentimental. And the closets above, with their carven doors, and the drawers below with their antique brass handles and lock-plates, so far from being empty, were uncomfortably full with articles of household garnishing or personal wear, made from home-grown, home-spun, home-woven, home-made material, linen or woollen. Much thereof might be the work of the bride's own deft, if toil-hardened fingers; but much, too, came of the many and heartily offered gifts of the neighbours and friends of the young couple. And it was once a thing of occasional occurrence rather than a custom that could be said to prevail, to place this wardrobe, so stored, on a wain – itself a gift like the rest, as well as the oxen which drew it – and convey it to the church at which the marriage ceremony was to be solemnised; making it a part of the wedding procession, in fact, and letting it stand by the church-door, or in the very porch,while the priest was fulfilling his function; and after the service to drag it thence to the future abode of the couple just made one. So by an easy transition of idea the wardrobe itself came to be called a bride-wain.

J.C. Atkinson

REVD JAMES ALDER WILSON, RECTOR OF CRATHORNE

OXEN AND CART, HELMSLEY

KILLED BY A BULL

. . . my grandfather Guy was killed with a bull, one he'd brought up himself. It was a Sunday morning, and me grandfather used to play the bass fiddle in Muker church. There was an orchestra in the church, them days: me grandfather played the bass, and there was a fiddle, and I wouldn't know whether they had drums or not, but they had four or five in orchestra. Well, me grandfather had put his best Sunday clothes on to go, and he passed this pasture where the bull was: and there was some heifers there, and he heard one of them in service, and he wanted to see which one it was. That was why he climbed over the wall, they think. And they always think that the bull didn't know him in his Sunday clothes, and that was why it gored him. Me father said he hadn't a rag left on him when they found him; it had gored him to death. He was a real good man, my grandfather, one of the best-living men there was: everybody said he wouldn't play a dirty trick on anybody. But the bull didn't know him in Sunday best.

Maggie Joe Chapman

NEDDY DICK'S MUSICAL STONES

. . . let me explain that among my reasons for visiting the head of Swaledale – near which stands the little village of Keld – was to meet a 'character' bearing the curious name of 'Neddy Dick.' . . . this remarkable person had made a musical scale with stones taken from the bed of the Swale, and how he could play tunes, pleasant to the ear, by striking them with a wooden mallet; that by means of a harmonium to which he had, with much ingenuity suspended a number of bells, carefully scaled, he was in the habit of producing remarkable, and often surprising effects; and that it was only to sympathetic listeners he cared to reveal his powers. As I have said, a strong reason for my visit to Keld, was to meet this ardent and untutored genius of the dale.

When within a mile or so of this village, I enquired of a passenger in the bus as to whether Neddy Dick was still living here . . . . The reply came, 'He is dead; he died quite a while back.' So to my disappointment, I was not destined to meet him, after all. However, I determined to learn more about him, and if possible, to see his ingenious musical instruments.

At the Cat Hole – a curious name for a neat comfortable inn – I made some enquiries about the musician of the mountains. I remarked to the landlady, Mrs. Hutchinson, that I had learned of his death. 'Yes,' said she, 'he died some two years ago; he left me his harmonium which is in one of the front rooms. His bells have gone to a relative at Skipton, and there is the clock – pointing to a 'Grandfather' standing on the staircase – whose bell Neddy so often asked for to complete his set.'

After tea I made my way down to the tiny hamlet to find out as to what had become of the musical stones. Here I had a further disappointment. The stones had, I was told, been

VILLAGE BAND, KELD

removed to an outhouse after Neddy became ill; and – pointing to a ruin – my informant said, 'The outhouse was demolished and the stones lie mixed up with the rubbish.' When the clearance takes place it is to be hoped that the stone dulcimer will be treated with respect.

Next morning I again visited this tiny hamlet numbering under fifty souls. I observed an empty house, and divined who had lived there. But to make sure, I asked a villager who was passing. 'Richard Alderson,' came the answer. 'Most of us knew him by the name of Neddy Dick.' Then my informant added gratuitously, 'He wer a queer un. He wer brought up to farming; but his mind was always running on music. He neglected himself badly; and though he had money he didn't know how to use it. Lots o' fowk came to hear him play on t'stones he had fished up out o' t'beck.'

Probably this man's estimate was that of the whole village. As I myself had not met Richard Alderson, it was not easy to judge of his true powers with anything like exactness; but a week later I was able to gain a much better estimate of the man from a cultured musician who had stayed in Keld during Neddy's lifetime. His account ran somewhat thus:

'During my visits to Swaledale I was much impressed by Alderson's musical ability. On his stones – which had been selected with the utmost care, and tuned by chipping – he rapped out many melodies with facility. His harmonium, with bells attached to a framework, made a happy combination. With one hand he played an accompaniment on the instrument; while with the other he chimed the melody on the bells. With this miniature orchestra he produced delightful effects, and charmed the many visitors who came to his cottage during the Summer months.'

J. Sutcliffe Smith

'DEAR OLD MEUCAR'

A certain writer bemoans a lack of power of musical expression and feeling in the dalesfolk of this and other adjacent places. Experience of 'German bands' or their like in places abroad must have spoilt the ear of this traveller; we, at any rate, cannot honestly concur in his opinion. Every village from Reeth to Keld has its 'band', the fame of whose attainments has spread far beyond the dales, though, we believe, there are those who detect nothing soul stirring in the skirl of the bagpipes. Apart from this, however, here before us is a most antiquated and primitive structure and over its lintel writ in large and ancient characters, so that even he who runs may read, the magical words 'BAND ROOM,' probably the smallest and most primitive Hall of Harmony in the kingdom.

As bearing on the notorious love of 'Swardal' folk for their home fastnesses, Richard Kearton, in his fine book, 'With Nature and a Camera' tells how he knew a little girl living high up Swaledale who was compelled to accompany her parents and reside in a Lancashire spinning town. One day some of her relations sent a round of fresh butter to them wrapped up in the cool-keeping leaves of the common Dock, whose large foliage tufts grow in plenty by the stony road and beck-sides from Thwaite to Reeth. 'The little girl's heart,' he writes, 'remained so true to the land of her birth, that she seized one of these (leaves) and cried, "let me kiss it, mother; it has come from dear old Meucar." '

Edmund Bogg

LEVISHAM VALLEY

The 'Corpse-way' from Keld to Grinton

Between the 'Cat-hole' and Greeness the old pack-horse track, or 'Corpse-way,' from Keld and Upper Swaledale passed over the summit of Mount Kisdon, and dropped down its eastern slope and crossed the Swale water half a mile or so north of Muker, kept along the moorland terrace high above the river and to north or it, and so on by Gunnerside to Barf-end, Low Row, Reeth, to its goal at Grinton. By those who know the district this ancient *via morti*, the green way of the Dead, can still be followed. Imagination pictures the many sad processions in 'thunder, lightening, snow, and in rain,' this ancient way has seen – the difficulties to be overcome, the weary pace in the short days of snow, a very nightmare of the Last Rites, to decently put away their beloved dead at the bidding of Faith! But, properly to understand the old route, the reader will have to forget the present good road to Richmond, which runs mostly along the south bank of the Swale. In the old days, before Macadam, there was no such road, so the old path and only one kept to the edge of the moor, along the limestone terrace as already indicated. The ancient trackway has been the witness of scenes both of joy and sorrow and hope – it was the wedding-party route, the christening route and the funeral route for all places west of Kisdon, a distance from Grinton's Mother Church of between twelve and sixteen miles. Sometimes as many as ten or a dozen couples on horseback, others afoot on 'shanks' galloway' would follow the cavalcade to Grinton – how different a scene to that when in after years, silently instead of with laughter

and gay speech, the same bodies, their life's labour over, were carried down for the last time to Grinton by their kith and kin. The corpse was borne on men's shoulders along this highway of the dead all the way to Grinton previous to interments being made possible at Muker, not in a wooden coffin but swathed in linen winding sheets, and enclosed in long wicker baskets laid upon a bier or carrier. It needs no violent stretch of fancy to look back through the years and years that have altered the manners and customs of the dale so much in some respects, and see the Funeral procession – a thin black line against the white carpeted ground, winding its way, sinuous-like, creeping with many a pause and twist up the slope and over the lonely Pisgah tableland of Mount Kisdon, and then down to the Swale and once more the upward toil to gain the terrace of Iveletside, and on over lonesome stony forest or heath land! A relay of bearers was absolutely necessary; at intervals there were stone seats or resting places along the route to place the trestle or carrier upon. A halt was invariably made opposite the 'Punch Bowl' at Feetham, where spiced hot ale and cakes and biscuits were served out to the bearers. From Feetham, refreshed in body if not in heart, the cortege toiled on with the body up Peat Gate and through Kearton, past Park Hall and John o' Gaunts to Reeth. Here, if not perhaps before, many of the villagers and the 'unbidden' would join the double file of mourners, and 'with sad steps and slow' to the chanting of a dirge, forward to the church, the 'Mother Church' to which all her children come back soon or late, and from the tower of which

BOLTON CASTLE

The bell of death beat slow −
It paused now, and now with rising knell
Flung to the hollow gale its sullen sound.

Edmund Bogg

THE THREAT OF 'COMING AGAIN'

. . . when a corpse is carried out of the house of death, it is invariably borne forth feet first, in order to prevent the dead person from 'coming again.' Nay, even in the days of hoary eld, it was a custom to whisper in the ear of the corpse that he was not to 'come again'; while, finally, there was the old practice of laying earth on the body, which was a heathen practice long before it was adopted in the Christian grave service . . .

An old woman who lived in Fryup, and whose chief celebrity depended upon the allegation that she kept the 'Mark's e'en watch,' and was able in consequence to foreshow the deaths of the coming year, one St. Mark's day, when she was questioned on the subject after her vigil, announced her own death as among the foredoomed ones, and assigned her reason for saying so. 'And,' she added, 'when I dee, for dee I s'all, mind ye carry me to my grave by t' church-road, and not all the way round by t' au'd Castle and Ainthrop. And mind ye, if ye de'ant, I'll come again.'

Now the church-road lay straight past her house to the foot of a very steep moor-bank, up which it went − and goes yet − with two zigzags. It is a stiff climb at any time, even when one has only himself and his coat to carry; but with a burden such as a coffin, with the grisly occupant inside, it is 'hosses' wark, not men's.' Well, the old lady died as she had predicted, and she died in a snowy time. And the difficulties of the church-road in a snowy time are almost intensely enhanced. I have gone both up and down the bank at such seasons, and speak with feeling. But the bearers faced the difficulties − perils, in a sense, they almost amounted to, − and waist-deep sometimes; still they persevered, and eventually got through with their undertaking and their burden. In plain words, they were ready to face anything; and many among them must have had such a day of toil and effort and fatigue as never before nor after fell to their lot; but they could not, dared not, face the chance of the old woman's 'coming again.'

J.C. Atkinson

A REPAIRABLE LOSS

Granny was a very clever woman, and very clean: but she was as hard as iron, nothing affected her. I remember hearing me grandad say, when she'd been called out to a confinement, 'What have you got, Margaret, this time?' And she just stood and said, 'I've got a bouncin' lad', she said, 'but it's deed.' Just as if a cat had lost kittens!' 'It's deed', she said, 'and thoo nivver saw sike a set [such a fuss] as she's makkin' in thee life − Lord, it's a repairable loss!' That's what they thought of losing babies, 'a repairable loss'. I should be only a little girl, and I didn't know what it meant, but it stuck in my mind.

Maggie Joe Chapman

UNLOADING COAL FROM THE *DIAMOND*

CHANGE IN CHARACTER OF THE PEOPLE OF STAITHES

A change has come over the inhabitants of Staithes since 1846, when Mr. Ord describes the fishermen as 'exceedingly civil and courteous to strangers, and altogether free from that low, grasping knavery peculiar to the larger class of fishing-towns.' Without wishing to be unreasonably hard on Staithes, I am inclined to believe that this character is infinitely better than these folk deserve, and even when Mr. Ord wrote of the place I have reason to doubt the civility shown by them to strangers. It is, according to some who have known Staithes for a long while, less than fifty years ago that the fisher-folk were hostile to a stranger on very small provocation, and only the entirely inoffensive could expect to sojourn in the village without being a target for stones. The incursion of the artistic hordes has been a great factor in the demoralization of the village, for who would not be mercenary when besought at all hours of the day to stand before a canvas or a camera? Thus, the harmless stranger who strays on to the staith with a camera is obliged to pay for 'an afternoon's 'baccy' if he want an opportunity to obtain more than a snapshot of a picturesque group. He may try to capture a lonely old fisherman by asking if he would mind standing still for 'just one second,' but the old fellow will move away instantly unless his demand for payment be readily complied with.

No doubt many of the superstitions of Staithes people have languished or died out in recent years, and among these may be included a particularly primitive custom when the catches of fish had been unusually small. Bad luck of this sort could only be the work of some evil influence, and to break the spell a sheep's heart had to be procured, into which many pins were stuck. The heart was then burnt in a bonfire on the beach, in the presence of the fishermen, who danced round the flames.

Gordon Home

RUNSWICK BAY

HOB'S HOLE AT RUNSWICK

Among the animals that feel the changes of the atmosphere the domestic cat is distinguished, and this, no doubt, has associated puss with witches and other storm-raising spirits. When the fishermen of Runswick are expected home, their wives and children, the better to ensure their safe arrival, exterminate the cats in the village and procure a fresh supply after the boats have returned. If the wind is unpropitious the children light a fire on the top of the cliff and dancing round it invoke the spirit of the storm in this way:–

> 'Souther wind, souther,
> And blow father home to my mother.'

Between the village and Kettleness Point, which ends Runswick Bay, stretching out between it and Sand's End, there is a cave in the alum rock. The tide fills this cave at high water; and it used to be regarded as the abode of a goblin called Hob; it is still called Hob's Hole. Wonderful stories were told of Hob, and how he was resorted to by mothers when their children suffered from whooping-cough. At low water the mother carried her child into the cave, and then in a loud voice evoked the goblin: 'Hob, Hob, Hob, mah bairn's getten kink-cough; tak' 't off, tak' 't off.'

The cave is seventy feet long and twenty wide at the mouth, and was once divided by a double natural column. Hob used to wander over the moors behind the bay with a lantern, and often decoyed travellers into the 'pots' to be found among the rocks, or else, in a driving night-storm of rain, would offer them shelter in his hole and leave them to perish by the incoming sea when the tide rose.

Thomas and Catherine Macquaid

NEVER SEEN THE SEA

It is extraordinary to notice the tenacity of the poor for stopping at home, while others like to boast of the countries they have seen, and the strange sights they have visited. I have known a woman of sixty, who had never moved out of the hamlet she had been born in, and never wished to do so. I have known a woman who lived at a village only a mile and a half from Filey Bay, who had never seen the sea.

At a tea for mothers, given at one of the two occasions of the late Queen's Jubilee, one mother was present who had not had her shoes on for fourteen years, or in other words had never gone outside her door.

That this tends to a fixed rigidity of outlook I do not deny, but as an old Latin tag reminds us, '*Cave ab homine unius libri*,' or, beware of the man of one book, for he is likely to know it thoroughly, so the man or woman who has never been away from his village is likely to be a storehouse of exact information.

Revd A.N. Cooper

DUNROBIN STRANDED AT SEATON

THE VIEW FROM WHITBY BRIDGE

One lingers on Whitby Bridge; the view of the harbour and its shipping is so quaint, with the wooden galleries and stairs, many-coloured in the sunlight. The broad quay west of the bridge is full of life of the most primitive kind; tall stalwart fishermen, red-bearded like their Danish forefathers – though some are dark with long eyes that gleam like those of a Breton – sit chatting on the rails till a bell sounds from the Staithes, the crowded flagged corner of the quay. A great heap of fish has been brought from the boats moored alongside, and the auctioneer is ready to put them up for sale. Hard-featured women, with shawls over their heads and tucked-up skirts, carry the fish in baskets placed on their heads up the slippery wooden steps that lead from the boats to the quay. They rarely raise a hand to steady their baskets as they walk, either to the flagstones where the auctioneer is standing, or to a group farther on, waiting with barrels of salt to strew over the shining loads they carry.

The sun was shining when we reached this scene, and the river was full of boats from Cornwall, Scotland, and elsewhere, their open hatchways, a dazzling display of colour, with heaps of fish glistening and shimmering like prism-tinted silver, while on the other side of us the quaint humour exchanged between the buyers and the auctioneer was most amusing. We saw a huge cod-fish sold for half-a-crown, and a hundred of herrings went for a few pence. The end of this walk beside the quay leads us to the west pier, stretching far into the sea; at the extreme end of this pier one gets a real idea of the sea, even when it is not very rough weather. We saw one gale at Whitby when no one could venture to the end of the pier, the waves dashed so furiously over it – clouds of spray were even flung over the lighthouses; it seems marvellous that either piers or lighthouses can withstand the force of the furious sea.

Thomas and Katherine MacQuaid

BY DOG CART TO BRANSDALE

We left Kirby, appearing to an outsider, to cut rather a comical figure; a large, tin trunk was to be the companion of the one who sat at the back of the dog-cart, tied on for security by the most available thing at hand, a *halter*. It kept its equilibrium well for some time, but when we got into the moorland ruts, and the cord became less tight with periodical jolts, it required as much coaxing and steadying as if it had been a drunken man.

By and by the road becomes so very rough and such hard work for the horse that we desire to alight and walk. The roads here are so constructed that at intervals we pass over a grip or channel which conveys the water across the road during heavy rains into a regular course, and so prevents much of the sandy road being washed away, which would otherwise cause inconvenience; to us they gave frequent shocks, for while our attention was directed right and left at any object of interest, there came such a violent shake, that for a moment we doubted whether we and our belongings had maintained our hold; to change sides of the road was a most difficult matter in case of meeting anything, or supposing it would be more comfortable to do so. One of the trio (rather timid) would much have preferred making her journey in one of the

BECKHOLE, GOATHLAND

broad four wheeled waggons most frequently seen on these roads.

Our guide had told us it was only six miles from Kirby Moorside to our destination in Bransdale, whilst our hostess had said ten; to us, the latter seemed nearer the mark, but our slow and laboured progress might make it appear longer than it really was.

Near our journey's end, still walking, we approached an old, dark, stone bridge, and beyond, a steep rise, which made us draw many a deep long breath.

We called to M— to direct us the road, and we would follow at leisure.

Watching the progress of our vehicle, we saw our driver had unconsciously dropped something which, as we neared, turned out to be some most important articles, umbrellas, portable seats, &c., strapped together; with these extra incumbrances we trudged along, at the same time thoroughly enjoying our novel position.

As we gained the summit of the hill, we rested a little, for our path had been rough and toilsome, but we were amply recompensed by the grand view spread around us; its vast extent; swelling hills, covered with deep, thick heather; a sky ever changing, illuming and shading, chasing away monotony from the scene, and carpeting the foreground, bright with the hues of pale, green mosses, or deep, rose-coloured patches of heath in flower.

Two Sunday School Teachers

'UP THE ASYLUM ROAD'

Our walks, taken twice a day, from 12 to 1 and from 2.30 to 3.30 (the rest of the day devoted to lessons in the schoolroom and to meals), were usually 'up the Asylum Road' where hedges and green fields and a few villas with gardens led up to the big iron gates and railings which flanked the entrance to the North Riding Asylum.

These walks brought us into early contact with the unfortunate inmates of that institution. We used to see gangs of men working in the fields under the supervision of their guards, who wore navy blue suits and peaked caps. They threw turnips into farm carts (it was before the sugar beet era), while from the road we stood to watch the rhythm of the performance and heard the 'Gee Wo!' and 'Ah Wey!' to the horse between the shafts. Sometimes a party of women lunatics would be met, chaperoned by keepers, taking the air; and some would laugh inanely and give us weird greetings, while others would walk along with bent heads, morose and devil-ridden. Small shawls formed the covering for their heads, from the confines of which the stricken faces would leer and peer at passers-by.

It was a distressing sight; and I can remember their noisome smell to this day.

Ethel, Lady Thomson

RUSTIC IDYLL

'STICKING NIGHTS'

On leaving school most boys went to what was called 'Farmplace' where a boy would have to work from 6 in the morning till darkness fell, living in, they received at the end of the year the princely sum of £5 out of this they had to buy their clothes etc. When they left home each boy would receive from his parents a 'bundle handkerchief' which contained his clothes. It was a blue and white checked linen cloth, I have one in my possession now. The girls sometimes went to 'farmplace' or they took 'situations' for the first year their wages being similar to the boys. The very poor and old people who were unable to work would get 2/- or 2/6 per week. The registrar came round on horseback to pay it. This came from the board of guardians. There was a lot of firewood carried out of Arncliffe and Limber woods. It was quite a common sight to see five or six mothers with some of their children on a fine summers day towards evening emerging from the wood carrying a load of stocks according to their size. The mothers carried the bundles on their heads. The

sticks they gathered would be roughly two inches in diameter and they called them oven sticks. These sticking nights I believe the women thoroughly enjoyed, it was a night out for them. They were not allowed to use axes or saws in the woods.

George Harland

THE NAMES OF THE FIELDS

I can still remember the names of the fields on the first farm I ever worked on, although it is seventy two years ago. They are as follows. The Cowpasture, High Park, Calf House Field, Newholm Field, The Carrs, Two Days Work, Five Days Work, Court Bank, Bream Field, The Stripe, The Clofts, The Horse Pasture, The Little Horse Pasture, The Well Field, Warton Field, Yak Field, Old Bank and Beacon Field.

George Harland

EAST AYTON SCHOOL, 1900

'MOISTURE STOOD LIKE PEAS ON THE WALLS'

When I went to school it was just one large room with a door on one side for the girls and one on the opposite side for the boys. There was no porch or cloakroom and the only furniture was the master's chair and desk, in which was kept the register and log book and other things, which made it very heavy. There was also a table with two drawers. The walls of the room were very damp and moisture stood like peas on the walls when the weather was muggy. The only heating was a stove in the centre of the room, with a smoke pipe going out of the roof.

One very cold winter the master had to drill us by marching us round the room in single file every fifteen or twenty minutes to keep us warm. This often happened and is recorded in the log book. When I started school, which was before I was five years old, the discipline was very bad. The boys were rough and there was many a fight which ended up with bleeding noses and black eyes. After a time a new master was appointed who soon altered all this by a liberal supply of flogging. The discipline soon became very good. There was strict silence in the school, only the masters voice could be heard or a scholar reading aloud. If the master saw any of us

with any toys out of our pockets we promptly got the stick. There was always two sticks on the master's desk which he bought at a little shop close to the school. One cane for the boys cost two pence and one for the girls cost one penny. Old John did a rattling good trade with his sticks and always had a bundle of these two sorts in stock. When any of us had done anything wrong there was a saying 'Though'll get twopenny for that'. We got caned if we were late in the morning or any other starting time. One character whom I shall call Bob was often late, he would be sent off from home at the proper time but found so many things to interest himself with, such as making sieve whips and potato guns, etc. He could not help it, it was in his make-up, but he got thoroughly flogged for it. His velvet coat was fluted with the cane marks on his back. On one occasion he was flogged for something which he had not done. When someone told the master that it had not been Bob who had done the mischief the master found this to be correct, so he compensated Bob with two pence for the mistake and by the look on Bob's face he was more than satisfied with the deal. I do believe he would have taken a flogging for that amount at anytime.

George Harland

64

THE SEAMER EXPRESS

THE WITCH AND THE HARE

Although we have heard it before, we hear over again with intense interest the story of the witch who brought constant ill-luck to a family in these parts. Their pigs were never free from some form of illness, their cows died, their horses lamed themselves, and even the milk was so far under the spell that on churning-days the butter refused to come unless helped by a crooked sixpence. One day, when as usual they had been churning in vain, instead of resorting to the sixpence, the farmer secreted himself in an outbuilding, and, gun in hand, watched the garden from a small opening. As it was growing dusk he saw a hare coming cautiously through the hedge. He fired instantly, the hare rolled over, dead, and almost as quickly the butter came. That same night they heard that the old woman, whom they had long suspected of bewitching them, had suddenly died at the same time as the hare, and henceforward the farmer and his family prospered.

Gordon Home

'SHOULD A HAIRY WORM CROSS YOUR PATH . . .'

It is commonly held that if you can find a four-leaved clover, and then walk backward upstairs to bed, sleeping with the leaf under your pillow, you will dream of the man you will marry.

It is considered most unlucky to see the new moon for the first time through glass. To break the spell cast upon you by such an unfortunate occurrence, make the sign of the cross on the doorstep, and jump backwards over it into the house.

Should a hairy worm cross your path, pick it up, throw it over your shoulder, and wish.

If you tread on an ordinary road beetle, rain will presently fall.

Whenever you hear a cuckoo, turn the money over in your pocket for luck.

To see a single magpie is very unlucky; two together is the reverse.

To see a single owl is also unlucky; but to hear one hoot, and then see it, foretells that you will have timely warning of some impending evil.

Wet your finger and cross your left shoe and wish every time you see a piebald horse.

Should two persons utter the same words at the same time, they must link their little fingers together and wish, keeping their wish secret.

The deciduous teeth of a male child, which have not touched the ground, if kept about the person are a specific against all manner of evil.

To ensure the child having a good and sound set of teeth, those which fall out of themselves, or which the child itself pulls out, should be dipped in salt and thrown into the fire.

A tooth found in a churchyard is believed to charm away

ELLERBY

the toothache if rubbed on the cheek.

And lastly, children's teeth must either be carefully preserved or utterly destroyed by fire with salt, as should one accidentally be swept away and fall into the ground, or be buried by some evil-minded person, the child will not live long, the first rites of ashes to ashes having been consummated.

No luck will follow a declaration of love if made on St. Dunstan's Day.

To be wed on St. Thomas's Day makes a bride a widow ere long.

Richard Blakeborough

'GOING TO THE LADIES'

I am old enough to remember when the 'social gatherings,' the dinner-parties of the day, met at 2 P.M., and sat with the wine before them, after the removal of the cloth, until six or seven o'clock in the evening, and sometimes later still, the guests being the country gentlemen, the parsons, and other 'professions'; some among whom were pointed out to my young mind for admiration as 'three-bottle men'; when 'going

to the ladies' meant more or less inability to drink any more, possibly even to remain on their chairs; and when nobody, not even the parson, was thought much the worse of because of such debauches (as they would be called now) as these.

J.C. Atkinson

HOW TO CURE WARTS

Wart-charmers are not defunct yet. I know several who, after pronouncing an inaudible incantation, rub the wart with a special stone, and then you are assured the wart or warts will die. Frog spit rubbed on a wart is said to be certain cure. If you rub your wart with a black snail and then place it on a thorn where you will never see it again, the wart, as the snail dies, will disappear. If you yearn to afflict anyone with warts, let them wash in water in which eggs have been boiled. This belief is quite common today. A plate of salt, upon which a dead man's hand has rested overnight, used to be considered good for chilblains.

Richard Blakeborough

SALTON GREEN

'SUNDAY'S BAIRN THRUFF LEYFE IS BLIST'

The future of a child greatly depends upon which day it is born.

> A Munday's bairn will grow up fair,
> A Tuesday's yan i' grace thruff prayer,
> A Wednesday's bairn 'ez monny a paain,
> A Tho'sday's bairn weean't bahd at heeam.
> A Friday's bairn is good an' sweet,
> A Settherday's warks frea morn ti neet,
> Bud a Sunday's bairn thruff leyfe is blist
> An' seear i' t' end wi' t' Saints ti rist.

From the day of its birth to that of its baptism, pepper cake, cheese and wine, or some other cordial, are offered to all those who cross the threshold. No one would think of refusing to 'tak a bite an' sup,' to wish the little stranger all the happiness and good luck possible. In many places, the doctor cuts the cake and cheese immediately after the happy event is over, giving a piece to every one present; neither cake nor cheese must have been previously cut into, and what is cut must be divided into just so many pieces as there are friends present, neither more nor less. Should it unfortunately happen the pieces exceed in number that of the guests, it would portend that troubles in his life will be too many to contend against; but should there be not enough pieces to go all round, then the child in after years will lack many of those comforts, the possession of which make life a blessing.

MASTER SUMMERSON, SALTBURN

DISPLAY OF TOYS AT MIDDLESBROUGH SCHOOL

When possible, a new arrival, before being laid by its mother's side, or even touched by her, is placed in the arms of a maiden. To a boy, this early contact, with our highest ideal of earthly purity, gives to him a nobleness of character which in after years will help the world to be better, whilst in the case of a girl she will grow up to be modest and pure in all things. The idea is pretty.

Richard Blakeborough

A COMPROMISE OVER CANING

Two boys who knew they were going to be caned for something which they were supposed to have done made their minds up that they were not going to be caned and would not hold out their hands.

One of them was soon flogged into submission, but the other one refused absolutely. The master caned him every morning for two weeks and he never did any lessons during those two weeks and had to stand at the top of the school beside the master's desk the whole of every day. But still he did not yield. The vicar was brought to talk to the boy, but he still refused to hold out his hand to be caned. At last a compromise was reached, and this was that if he would hold out his hand it would not be caned, which he did and was sent to his desk to resume his lessons.

George Harland

VILLAGE SCHOOLMASTER, RUNSWICK

SOMEWHERE IN RYEDALE

ARMSTRONG THE TURF CUTTER

Armstrong is turf cutting. He is the handy man of the farm and lives at a picturesque thatched cottage near by. He is a genial son of the dale, and is familiar with every nook and cranny in the length and breadth of Bilsdale, and can relate no end of stories touching on the district. He can cut turf, ring a pig, set a mole or a rat trap, beat for game, cut a turf or make a rook, and, in fact, as we have said, turn his hand to anything pertaining to a farm. He is as straight as a poplar, and his long spells of exposure to the open air have bronzed his face to a good standing colour.

To-day the turf is too hard for him to cut such a thickness as he would like. The implement for cutting is similar in shape to a hay spade, though smaller, except that it is turned up about two inches on one side. The spade is six feet in length and has a wooden cross arm at the end for pushing with the hands. The turf cutter fixes round the waist what are called 'Nappers,' a V shaped piece of hard wood, about two inches thick, fastened round the body with strong cord or leather, for protection's sake, as in cutting a turf the whole body is pushed forward with the wooden cross arm of the implement pressing against the 'nappers.' Being desirous of cutting a turf, we fix on the apparatus and cut *one* turf and feel quite satisfied with the effort made. The next business is to 'rook' the turves, otherwise to place them in cocks to dry; under the directions of skipper Armstrong we build a rook and were much gratified on our return visit two months later, to learn that it had not fallen, but had stood intact till harvested.

Michael Heavisides

DREADFUL TEMPEST AT THWAITE

At times the raging elements have nearly succeeded in ravaging and razing Thwaite to the ground, carrying much bodily away. This was the case half a dozen years ago, when a terrific thunderstorm and cloud-burst swept down from Shunnor, and every evil spirit of earth and sky seemed to have been let loose: as one dalesman put it, 'It cam i' twa gert pushes.' One, Broderick of Hawes, with a keen eye for natural phenomena, observed on the morning of this great flood, which nearly destroyed Hardraw and Thwaite, what possibly gives the clue to the cause of this dreadful tempest. There was an ominous silence before the furies of the air were let loose, and then the triple storm began. There were *three tiers* of discharging thunder-clouds, one above the other, moving slowly northwards over the heights between Simonstone and Thwaite; had the awful bombardment of the land *lasted five minutes* longer both places would have been doomed – wiped off the map! As it was, great numbers of cattle and sheep were lost, houses, laithes, walls innumerable were thrown down, and a vast amount of property swept away. David Calvert lost nearly all his stock of carts and implements, and only escaped drowning by what seemed a miracle. The dwellings of Thwaite were flooded several feet, and the little sheltered vegetable and flower gardens of the place were wrecked, despoiled of all they held, roots and seed being carried away from the plots here to beautify nooks and corners next year at lower levels!

Edmund Bogg

THWAITE

THE BLACKSMITH AT THWAITE

. . . we soon come in sight of Thwaite, and from the brow of the last hill we can hear distinctly the ring-ring, clang, ring! of the blacksmith's hammer at the smithy by the brig and inn (which he keeps), but there is no 'spreading chestnut tree' shading his 'smiddy' here. In other respects David Calvert is a wholesome example of the village Smith – long may their race last! A broad chested, strong and clear-eyed man is he, with large and powerful arms, blacksmith and publican to boot, being also the landlord of the 'Joiners' Arms.' Here both beast and man can be fed and the horse shod after a trying or prolonged tramp over the hills from Hawes or Kirkby Stephen. This inn will be found 'a home from home' truly, a place to leave with regret, and come again to, with expectations that will not be disappointed, after many days, so long as the present home-rule prevails there at the motherly hands of Mrs. Calvert and her daughter.

Edmund Bogg

THE SMITHY AT YEARBY

. . . in a short time I passed by the little village, Yearby, and its little school with the well-kept garden in front. A little further on, on the other side of the road is the blacksmith's shop – an ideal village smithy, snugly reposing under the shade of a magnificent tree, which, for the poet's sake, we will hope is a chestnut. How musical the regular ding, BANG – ding, ding, BANG – ding, ding, BANG! as the skilful master-blacksmith indicates with his small hammer the part he requires smiting with the big sledge-hammer so easily wielded by that leather-aproned, muscular youth. The village forge! – almost *any* village forge – with its glowing flame of roaring fire, the brilliant sparks shooting from the work on the anvil, which sparks the hardy smith heeds no more than splashes of cold water; the little lads leaning against the door-post, eagerly watching; the prosperous look of plenty of work on hand – grouped about the door a medley collection of ploughs, carts and wheels, a reaper, and other agricultural implements – what a picture all this makes.

'Q. T.'

EXCURSION TO THE FORGE VALLEY

THE DOCTOR'S 'FLYING MACHINE'

It was not until 1911 that my Father bought a car and, even
then, the invasion of the coach house by a machine was
regarded with some doubt, and the gig still stood forlornly in
the yard, 'in case'. But finally it seemed 'the thing' would
actually go, though break downs were frequent, and the
chauffer spent a large part of his time in 'churning her up wi'
t' handle', mending tyres, and re-mending them in summer
when the heat lifted the patches, 'hotting her up' or 'making her
give ower boiling'; and, 'through time' these temperamental
difficulties were overcome. But to the end of his days, my
Father would always lean forward when ascending hills, 'to
throw the weight on to the horse's back'.

Many of the patients had never seen a motor car before and,
in some cases, were thoroughly alarmed, and dare not even
venture forth to call the Doctor in as he passed by, for fear of
'happening an accident'; and the following letter is an example
of this caution.

> Mr. English, Sir,   January 25th 1912
>
> Please excuse my neglect, as we have expected to see you
> pass, which we have, but in a Flying Machine, so not able to
> call you.
>
> Yours truly

Brenda H. English

STAINTONDALE

THE DOBSON BROTHERS, YARM

RICHMOND

TOBOGGANING AT RICHMOND

One of the liveliest of all my recollections is of the terrific winter of 1895. There was splendid tobogganing for weeks on the long three mile hill down from Catterick. A zest was added to it by the fact that in the Borough of Richmond the sport was forbidden. On the other hand only the last hundred yards or so of the hill was in Richmond. The rest was in another parish, I presume Catterick.

We could toboggan in peace therefore up to a certain gate where two policemen were stationed to maintain the law. The thing to do was to glide up to the expectant officers and stop under their noses. If you were going too fast and could not stop you threw yourself off: they seized the toboggan and you went home and made another out of soap boxes.

John Stuart Hodgson

'FAG' TO CONAN DOYLE'S BROTHER

I was 'fag' in my first term at Richmond to Innes Doyle, the brother of Conan Doyle, the famous inventor of Sherlock Holmes. He was a big cheerful individual who afterwards became a guardsman and went to Pekin with the Boxer punitive expedition and brought back with him the first Pekinese ever, I believe, imported into this country. Long years afterwards, I attended a seance with Conan Doyle at Putney. A voice claiming to be the spirit of Innes Doyle, who

had died a year or two before, spoke to me. 'You are Innes Doyle?' I asked. 'Yes' muttered the voice, 'You remember Richmond?' 'Yes.' 'Do you remember anything peculiar about it?' Silence. 'Come, don't you remember anything peculiar about the School Chapel, for instance?' (I need not say that there is no boy who ever went to Richmond who does not remember the School Chapel which had shops underneath it, the only one of its kind I believe, in the country). 'Grrr' said the voice suddenly; and after that it would say no more. I am sure the whole thing was a mere ventriloquist exhibition on the part of the medium. He had found out that I had been at Richmond and got caught in his own craftiness.

John Stuart Hodgson

THE CIRCUS VISITS RICHMOND

There is a sleepy quietness about this way up from the [Richmond] station, which is quite a short distance, and we look for much movement and human activity in the wide space we have reached; but here, too, on this warm and sunny afternoon, the few folks who are about seem to find ample time for conversation and loitering. At the further end of the great square there are some vast tents erected close to the big obelisk that forms the market-cross of the present day. Quantities of straw are spread upon the cobbles, and the youth of Richmond watches with intense interest the bulgings of the canvas walls of the tents. With this they are obliged to be

WEIR AND CHURCH, THORNTON-LE-DALE

content for a time, but just as we reach this end of the square two huge swaying elephants issue forth to take their afternoon stroll in company with their son, whose height is scarcely more than half that of his parents. The children have not waited in vain, and they gaze awe-struck at the furrowed sides of the slate-gray monsters as they are led, slowly padding their way, across the square. We watch them as they pass under the shadow of Holy Trinity Church, then out in the sunshine again they go lurching past the old-fashioned houses until they turn down Frenchgate and disappear, with the excited but respectful knot of children following close behind.

Gordon Home

A CHILD'S 'PARTY PIECE'

Lessons and walks over for the day, we had tea, changed our dresses and spent an agonizing hour in the drawing-room. We were trained like dogs at the circus, having to sit on our separate chairs, without any toys or books, not allowed to speak unless spoken to, and certainly forbidden to 'fidget'. Occasionally, however, this penal servitude was varied if the parents wished to impress a visitor with the talents of their offspring. In 1885 the country had been shocked by the fate of General Gordon, so, without being told why or wherefore, we

were taught to sing a sort of dirge in unison, standing side by side in a row and voicing this sentimental regret:

'Too late, too late to save him!
Too late in vain he cried . . .'

We did not find out for some years after who 'he' was, nor why he could not be saved from a fate of which we were completely ignorant.

Ethel, Lady Thomson

ICEBERGS ON BUTTERTUBS PASS

For some weeks after the great storm of 1895 the roads between Swale and Yoredale were impassable to wheeled vehicles, and for several weeks no market could be held at Hawes, few or nobody to attend with stock to sell! Walls of snow from twelve to sixteen feet in height barred the way over Buttertubs pass; and as in the previous long frost and great snowfall of 1885–6, after the roads were 'opened,' that is dug out, great iceberg-like or hewn marble blocks of frozen snow rested at intervals along the highways either side of the road.

Edmund Bogg

SCHOOL PARTY AT LEYBURN

ECCENTRIC TEACHERS

It is the foreign masters curiously who live most clearly in my mind. There was an Alsatian called Kessler, who looked like a Cruikshank caricature and went always accompanied by one of those spotted dogs then called carriage dogs. His predecessor was a little man called Hessenberg, who attained fame by walking up the Chapel aisle with the end of a string of sausages hanging out of his pocket. The last was a big Swiss, the hairiest man I ever saw. Swimming in the water he looked like a bear, he was so completely covered with long dark hair. He was rather a surly individual, and doubtless we tried him hard. He had a box of geological specimens on his desk before him, and when wrath, was wont to exclaim as a sort of war-cry, 'I will throw a mineral at you.'

John Stuart Hodgson

'PLEASE, SUR, WE AR'N'T LASSES'

The inspectors of our Board schools can recount many true and curious anecdotes of our country scholars; but it should be borne in mind by the department that, although the Yorkshire country-people and their bairns are bilingual, it is only their mother tongue and ordinary English which up to the present they have mastered. The southern twang, pronunciation, and slang is to them as a mystic rune. North-country men, if you please, to examine North-country boys and girls. Very often the questions, as put by South-country inspectors, might just as well be asked in Sanskrit, and very naturally they remain unanswered, whilst the class is voted as hopeless dunces, when the fault really lies at the door of the questioner. At one school in Wensleydale a South-country inspector, when examining a class on the Bible, put this question, 'Neow tell me something abeout Mouses.' 'Cats kill 'em,' was the prompt reply. Another one said to a promising standard in mental arithmetic, 'Three packets of pins at a penny each, five hanks of tape penny each, nine reels of thread penny each, five boxes of hair-pins penny each, and six ounces of worsted at three halfpence per ounce. How much does the parcel come to? Quick!' But the speed with which the question had been asked, the twang, and the unfamiliar sound of many of the words, left the standard almost in absolute ignorance of the question. One thing, and of only one thing, were they clear upon – that they were being asked something about *thread*, *worsted*, and *hairpins*. But as the inspector uttered that 'Quick!' he fixed his eyes on one lad, and the effect of that glare was mesmeric.

The lad immediately answered, 'Please, sur, we ar'n't lasses'.

Richard Blakeborough

HEADMASTER, FAMILY AND HIS STAFF, GREAT AYTON

FOXTON'S LIVERY STABLES, SCARBOROUGH

'A BLINND HOSS AN' A BLINND JOCKEY'LL *NIVVER DEEA*, HOOIVER'

The story runs that he set off for Doncaster for the Leger . . . and, carrying his boots and saddle on his back, applied for admittance to the paddock. He was then unknown, and as he could not give the name of any employer and had no engagement to ride he was refused admittance. But Jim was not to be baulked. He had come in the hope of getting a ride, and was not going to allow the gateman to spoil his chance. So he walked on to the moor and got someone there to help him – for he was only the height of sixpenno'th o' copper – over the railings into the holy of holies. Here fortune favoured the bold, for someone who had seen him at the little country meetings gave him a chance mount. This began his career, which was so brilliant, and might have been so much more so had he only had greater restraint over himself.

The bottle was his besetting evil, yet many of the northern owners and trainers would rather have him up on their fancied horses, even when he was obviously three sheets in the wind, than many other jockeys with reputations, who were his contemporaries. The late Mr. 'Josh' Radcliffe, who knew him well, says: –

'So bad was his state at times that it is marvellous how he retained his seat in the excitement of a race, and still more to win as he often did. He took his occasional moral "fits" after an orgy, and accompanied by his ever-watchful and lifelong pal, Nat Outred, would go for a long pedestrian "spell" over the Yorkshire moors for days together. Thus recuperated in mind and body he would turn up at York or Doncaster in cherry-ripe condition. "They can leeak oot for Jim noo," Nat would say. True enough, the best of his rivals *had* to "look oot" when he was fit. On one occasion he was "far gone" when engaged to ride one of "Paddy" Drislane's horses. Fearing that he would not be able to steer the horse, "Paddy" furnished a hood and blinkers as a safeguard. Jim, on coming to his mount, saw the curtain. "Naay, naay! tak' it awaay, tak' it away . . . a blinnd hoss an' a blinnd jockey 'll *nivver deea*, hooivver."'

J. Fairfax-Blakeborough

RIDING THE 'TIT'

Jim Snowden's first riding experience was as a very little boy, when his parents, who were nomadic hawkers, with possibly a

THE ZETLAND MEET AT MIDDLETON LODGE

gypsy strain in their blood, were en route from fair to fair in Yorkshire and Lincolnshire. He had to ride some of the horses they had bought, or 'swopped,' bareback from one fair to another, and then show off their points (still bareback) . . . . This gave him dash, daring, grip and a knowledge of queer-tempered animals which later stood him in good stead. Occasionally, some of the gypsy fraternity, with which Yorkshire and Lincolnshire at that time abounded, got hold of a blood 'un with a turn of speed, and entered it at some of the many flapping meetings thenadays held all over the country, and in connection with every village feast. It was Jim Snowden whom they used to seek to ride their 'tit,' and in this way he got quite a lot of practice, and was up to not a few dodges before ever he thought of going in for the Turf as a profession.

J. Fairfax-Blakeborough

THE DUKE OF LEEDS AT HOUNDS

After a lapse of eighty years, a Duke of Leeds was once more ready to keep hounds. This time, not to hunt in the 'far west' and run into Westmoreland, but to take command of the now well established 'Bedale.'

A more fitting person could not have been found. As a large land and covert owner, devoted to all field sports, and especially fond of a quick gallop over a good country, he was the very man for the position, and he came into office with the goodwill and the best wishes of all.

In addition to the regulation three days a week, the Duke kept a sufficient number of hounds to enable him to hunt a fourth; on which he hunted hounds himself, devoting this day to the west, north-west, and south-west sides of the country, where he had some good sport.

Those who are fond of hounds, and take an interest and pride in the pack they regular hunt with, owe a very great debt of gratitude to the Duke.

Frank H. Reynard

DIARY OF THE BEDALE HOUNDS

1898. On the 26th November, there was a good and hard day's sport in the southwest part of the country. . . .

On the 12th December I should think a poultry stealer was killed.

Found in Limekiln Wood. After a circular hunt of about twenty-five minutes, the fox took refuge on the roof of a cottage in Catterick. Being dislodged from here, he bolted through the open door of the first cottage he came to, and the huntsman going in with a couple or two of hounds, he met his death on the floor of the 'front parlour,' much to the delight of the inhabitants of Catterick.

On the 13th January, there was a capital gallop from Langton Hall.

Frank H. Reynard

AT THE SMITHY, RYEDALE

BOILED SWEETS FOR A 'CLOD'

We often stopped at the 'blacksmith's shop' to watch Charlie Snowden hammering away, sparks flying and shoes sizzling hot being fitted to the smoking smelly hoof with a 'haud up! stand still! give ower!' and old Ben sweating in the corner – up and down, up and down, blowing the bellows and making funny faces at us lads. There were always horses being shod, from trap ponies and galloways and hunters to heavy farm horses – Clydesdales and Shires. Most of the tradesmen had horses and carts – four wheeled trolleys, though butchers usually went on their rounds with a two-wheeled dog cart, a high one, maybe to frustrate the dogs, of which there seemed to be hundreds. The roads were adequately spattered with horse manure – 'hoss-muck.' The roadmen with their barrows were kept busy despite the willing help of numerous lads with buckets and fire shovels, who helped to fertilise the many gardens and allotments. I think the standard charge per bucketful was a penny, though sometimes there was a glut on the market and a 'meg' was as much as you could get. A penny was a 'clod'; a halfpenny a 'meg.' This helped out the weekly stipend, usually a penny. On a Saturday morning, pay-day, with a copper or two in our pockets, we went round the shops. Maybe one 'clod' went on boiled sweets (fourpence a pound) or monkey nuts, same price, or perhaps we went to old Ma Clements. Now there was a miscellany indeed to gladden the heart and excite action; goodies in glass bottles, tins and cardboard boxes, jumbled up with sweet locust beans, licorice root, pea-shooters with split peas for ammunition, potato guns, pistols with caps that cracked off, square elastic for catapults – in short everything that a red-blooded lad could wish for.

Maurice E. Wilson

79

THE VILLAGE STORE, LASTINGHAM

TREACLE FOR 2D. A POUND

There was three grocers in the village, two of these employed an apprentice who always had plenty of work to do as nearly everything was weighed out in the shop. There was very little packaged stuff, perhaps only soap and blacking for shoes, or black lead for polishing on the firesides and ovens. A machine was used for cleaning the currants and another one for grinding the coffee. The shelves in the shop were packed with large cannisters about two feet high and fifteen inches in diameter which were marked with the groceries they contained. There were three different kinds of flour always kept in stock. There was also a drum of treacle which had a lever tap attached to it so that the treacle could be cut off immediately. Treacle was then two pence per pound. The groceries were delivered to the farm in spring carts.

George Harland

THE NOTED BANANA SHOP, YORK

CROSBY'S MANSION, HUTTON BUSCEL

LIVING IN A DEN

. . . on occasion of some official inquiry as to the ways in which the working classes were housed, I received an invitation from the then Vicar of Egton (Ishmael Fish) to go down thither to meet the Commissioner, and to assist in the inquiries he wished to make . . . We first went to a small farmhouse, which has since been entirely rebuilt by the present owners of the estate, wherein the commonest rules of decency were not, and could not be, attended to as regarded the sleeping arrangements. We then went to two cottage dwellings in the main street of the village or (one of them) hardly out of it. As entering from the street or roadside, we had to bow our heads, even although some of the yard-thick thatch had been cut away about and above the upper part of the door, in order to obtain an entrance. We entered on a totally dark and unflagged passage. On our left was an enclosure partitioned off from the passage by a boarded screen between four and five feet high, and which no long time before had served the purpose originally intended, namely, that of a calves' pen. Farther still on the same side was another dark enclosure similarly constructed, which even yet served the purpose of a henhouse. On the other side of the passage opposite this was a door, which on being opened gave admission to the living room, the only one in the dwelling. The floor was of clay and in holes, and around on two sides

were the cubicles, or sleeping-boxes . . . of the entire family. There was no loft above, much less any attempt at a 'chamber'; only odds and ends of old garments, bundles of fodder, and things of that sort. And in this den the occupants of the house were living! And the other place we went into was no better. The Commissioner seemed 'satisfied';at least he did not desire to carry on his investigations any farther.

This was at Egton. Now let me tell some of my experiences nearer home. I made a fierce onslaught, when I first came to the place, on the shameful immorality of the usages and manners I found prevalent here. The resident Wesleyan minister wished me God-speed, and hoped I would persevere, adding that his own hands and tongue were tied by reasons of certain relations affecting his position. One of my most respectable inhabitants, himself a leading Wesleyan, also came to me, equally wishing me God-speed, but adding, 'But you must not stop here, Mr. Atkinson; you must go a bit farther yet,' and when I pressed him to speak out, and explicitly, he said, 'You must go in at the landlords and put it upon them to give us better-arranged houses to live in. I want to keep my servants decent. But how can I when, doing all I can, I have to let my men farm-servants go through the women-servants' room, or else, just the other way, the girls through the men's apartment?'

Nay, one day, when as little expecting anything of the kind as to be called upon to say 'Nolo episcopari,' on occasion of a

visit to Kilton Castle, I entered the farmhouse on the Liverton side, to greet my old friends who lived there and permitted the stabling of my horse, and the woman of the house said to me (in direct reference to my 'onslaught' aforesaid), 'Would you mind coming upstairs with me, and seeing for yourself how our sleeping-place is arranged!' Of course I went, and what I found was one long low room, partitioned off into four compartments nearly equal in size. But the partitions were in their construction and character merely such as those between the stalls in a stable, except that no gentleman who cared for his horses would have tolerated them in his hunting or coaching stable. These four partitioned spaces were no more closed in the rear than the stalls in an ordinary stable, and the partitions were not seven feet, hardly six and a half in height, while the general gangway for all the occupants was along the open back. The poor woman said to me, as she showed me the first partition, allotted to her husband and herself and their two youngest children, the next to their children growing rapidly up to puberty, the third to the farm-girls, and the fourth to the man and farm-lad, 'How can I keep even my children clean when I can only lodge them so?'

J.C. Atkinson

ROASTING FEATHERS IN THE OVEN

Oh, it could be bitter cold in winter-time, even inside your house: you see, we'd just have a coal or peat fire, there was no central heating, and not many stoves. I'll tell you how cold it could get. We had no inside lavatory, of course, so we had a 'jerry' each, all on us: well, in cold snowy weather, I've seen all those jerries frozen over – so she's been a bit cold i' that bedroom, hasn't she! But we always had plenty of blankets on, and we cuddled up.

And we always had good beds. Now me mother was *most* particular on a *good bed*, a very good bed: never nothing raggy on wir beds, but good blankets, good sheets and a feather mattress, what we called a feather bed. They were home-made, you know, from our own goose feathers, because we used to do a lot o' geese for Christmas. After you'd plucked your geese, Mother used to roast all feathers in the oven, and then we had to clean 'em all. That was a job, them blooming feathers! We used to do it in the outhouse, and the small feathers just had their ends cut off: but the big ones, you had to pull 'em off pens [quills] this way, and then that way, to just get the feathery parts off. They were lovely beds, but, oh, they took *ages* to stuff.

Maggie Joe Chapman

DOUBLE-SIDED GRAVESTONES

At the moorland sidings or funerals as an almost universal rule no expense was spared or grudged, even by the most miserly and thrifty. My astonishment was all the greater when in one moorland churchyard I found that several families had 'paired' for gravestones, one family using one face and the other the reverse.

R.W.S. Bishop

SOUTH BAY, SCARBOROUGH

A VISIT TO SCARBOROUGH BEACH

Sometimes when we left the hotel we would set our course for the sands; two little boys in sailor suits, equipped with buckets, spades and shrimping nets. Through the station yard with the horse drawn waggonettes and the sweet smell of horse dung, down the valley and along the valley road to the sea; passing a line of one-horse phaetons drawn by horses driven by postillions dressed in faded jockey costumes; on to the sands and along the sands below the walls of the Spa promenade, to our destination. The Children's Corner, the place where the so-called 'best children' played. In those days Scarborough was a very class conscious town. 'The best people' resided on the South Cliff, tradesmen and shopkeepers lived and worked in the centre of the town, the lodgings and boarding houses were mostly on the North Side.

On the front the divisions were marked by the Spa, the exclusive resort of the prosperous and respectable with a sprinkling of the aristocracy; in the centre the foreshore where the cheap restaurants and fun palaces catered for the day trippers; and the final barrier of the Castle Hill between the South Bay and the North Bay which catered mainly for the boarding house trade.

Presumably we were taken to The Children's Corner south of the Spa so that we could mix with our betters. If the tide came in when we were at The Children's Corner the only way back was over the Spa; the usual entrance fee to the Spa was sixpence but children trapped by the tide were allowed over on payment of a penny toll. It was an ordeal passing over the Spa, past the bandstand and through the well dressed throng, where scruffy children with buckets and spades were clearly out of place. But there was a treat in store at the north end of our passage across the Spa. Here we could look down and enjoy Catlin's Pierrots performing on their small canvas-covered stage set upon the sands immediately below. Will Catlin, the leader of the troupe, was a hero to Charles; someone larger than life, flamboyant, full of infectious energy. The Pierrots were dressed in voluminous white jackets and trousers, decorated with large black bobbles and wearing a white pointed felt hat adorned with a black bobble on the side. We could never see enough of them, especially Charles, who gave imitations of Will Catlin singing his favourite song – 'Here comes the galloping Major'.

Tom Laughton

SCARBOROUGH BEACH

'SHE'S NOT A LADY, SHE'S AN ACTRESS'

The highlight of the social week in Scarborough was the Sunday church parade on the South Cliff promenade. The well-dressed congregations emerged from the fashionable churches after the eleven o'clock services and congregated on the Esplanade, all walking sedately to display their finery. It was the only occasion on which father and mother would take us out together. We would cross the penny toll bridge over the valley to join the awesomely respectable throng. Charles used to tell the story how on one of these occasions he noticed a particularly well dressed and attractive young woman. Pulling mother's hand he excitedly pointed to her saying 'Look mother, look at the pretty lady!' Mother gave one quick glance – 'Hush Charlie – look the other way, she's not a lady, she's an actress.'

Tom Laughton

FRESH OYSTERS, SCARBOROUGH

84

'LOOK TO YOUR DRAINS AND CHIMNEYS'

Local peculiarities in the matter of customs and feasts exists, as might be expected, to a considerable extent. Thus, for instance, at Helmsley there is still held once a year what is called the *Vardy Dinner*. In the days before the Government appointed sanitary officers, Helmsley elected its own local committee to inspect the town once a year as regards sanitary matters. In the evening the inspectors met, supped, discussed, and gave their 'verdict'. Hence *Vardy Dinner*. The form, I am told, is still kept up, but chiefly for social purposes. The dinner is held annually, the committee having earlier in the day gone through the form of walking through the main streets, scrutinising at least the outside of dwellings as they pass. The Helmsley folk jokingly warn one another on this important day thus – 'Look to your drains and chimneys.'

A custom with a somewhat similar intention used to take place at Kilburn immediately before the village feast, which there is held on the Saturday after Midsummer Day. A man was dressed up to represent the Lord Mayor of York, and another to represent the Lady Mayoress. These two were then dragged through the village street in a cart by lads. As they went along they recited a doggerel and visited all the houses of the place, exhorting the people to tidy their gardens, trim their hedges, and make their tenements look generally respectable for the feast; in the event of these orders being disregarded a mock fine was imposed.

Revd M.C.F. Morris

'TEGATTENLAADSITWINNER'

A Frenchman once said to me, 'I could understand you English people, if you did not speak so quickly'. Aye, just so, and so would many another body from other counties understand a great deal of what our country folk say if each word was uttered separately, but with us, as in standard English, very frequently no pause is made between commas; so the difficulty increases tenfold, when a stranger strives to follow a fairly classical dalesman or woman. Take, for instance, a few words which the other day I heard a woman shout across a village street to her daughter. Firstly, as they sounded when uttered, then the same as they would be written, and thirdly, the translation.

As spoken. Teggattenlaadsitwinner.

As written. T' egg 'at t' 'en laad's i' t' winner.

Standard English. The egg (that) the hen laid is in the window.

Richard Blakeborough

PICKERING

'T'AWD GANG' MINER

Another interesting 'old inhabitant' is George Reynoldson, now in his 83rd year, who began work at the age of ten as a miner at 'T'awd Gang' mine, wherein he toiled for 63 years. George was summoned to London as a witness in regard to certain Shooting Rights – an action between the Lord of the Manor and the Broderick family, yeomen of Spring End and Summer Lodge. . . . To some question put by the judge to Reynoldson, anent shooting, he is said to have answered, 'Yer honour, it isn't shutting noo-a-days, its on'y modder (murder)! When ah were a lad, gentlemen used to shut ower points (pointer-dogs) – that's wat a'call spoort. Noo-a-days, t'gents hire men to draave birds tit guns, which is nowt at all but modder.' George clearly proved a tough nut for the London barristers to crack – 'no gowk, but real Swaddle.' During his cross-examination he replied, hand to ear, 'A's varry deaf – ye mun speak up – ah ave already said all at ah noo t' t'other side, an' ye heeard it all, an' a've nowt else to tell ye.' To the writer's question, 'And what did you think of London?' he made answer, 'Ah reckon nowt at all aboot Lunnon – they're onny pupheeads there; it's a faane place eneaf, bud theer's sadly too mich sparkling abaat. Kristle Pallace is a faane place, an' might dea (do) well eneaf. There was lots a portraits of kings and queens' which seems to have pleased the old fellow mightily; but 'the finest place on earth' to

George's thinking is Melbecks Moor and T'awd Gang Mines!

Edmund Bogg

THE 'SOCIETY HUMORIST'

I remember on one occasion, when being driven to the station by a real old Yorkshire coachman – I had been one of a house party for three days as society humorist – the old fellow giving me a huge dig with his elbows, and saying, 'Ah saay, is yon all you deea fer a living?' 'That is all,' I replied. 'Well, by goa! bud ya git yer living easy, you deea.' 'I don't know; if you had all the knocking about that I have perhaps you would not think it quite so easy,' said I. 'Whya, Ah deean't knaw; what ya'll 'ev yer expenses paid, 'evn't ya?' 'Certainly,' I answered. 'Aye; an' ya git fed fer nowt, deean't ya?' 'Of course,' I replied, greatly amused. 'Whya then,' said he, 'Ah'll tell ya what: ya travel fer nowt, yer sheltered fer nowt, fed fer nowt, an' ya deea nowt; Ah leeak upon ya ez nowt i' t'wo'lld else bud a aristocratic pauper.' 'Wait a moment,' said I; 'don't you think brains count for something in a matter of this kind?' And then, with that ineffable scorn which I think only the Yorkshireman of that type can assume, he said, 'Braans! braans!! braans!!! Ugh, Ah've ez monny brains ez you 'ev if they war nobbut scraped oot.'

Richard Blakeborough

FLOODS AT YORK

ORIGINAL POETRY ON THE YEAR OF OUR LORD, 1895

July next came, as all's aware
'Twas two days rain for one day fair;
The thunder rolled, the lightning flashed,
And down the valley the water splashed,
And such a waste amongst the hay
For many a load was washed away.

When August came it was so bright
The sun it shone from morn till night,
And all things round they looked so pleasant,
A smile was on both lord and peasant.

The next that came was rich September,
And such a month none can remember,
There was such a hot and clear sky,
The corn was all secured dry.

John Magginson

FIRE AT VICTORIA HOTEL, RICHMOND

RICHMOND CASTLE AND BRIDGE

FIRE AT THE VICTORIA HOTEL

The Victoria Hotel was in Finkle Street on the site occupied now by Cooper and Leatherbarrows, the hairdressers and Richmond Cleaners. On April 1st, 1908, fire broke out in the hotel.

At that time the Fire Brigade was made up of volunteers, most of them tradesmen in the town and workmen in the vicinity. When there was a fire, the fire-bell was rung from the clock tower which summoned the volunteers.

At 37 Market Place lived volunteer fireman Bill Ascough. On this April morning he was awakened round about 5.30 a.m. by a loud knocking on the side door, and after a few minutes got up and put his sleepy head out of the window, and asked what the row was about.

One of the other firemen a Mr Kinchin, stood below, and he shouted up that the Victoria Hotel was on fire and they were to get round there as quickly as possible. There was a slight pause and Bill shouted down, 'Oh so the Victoria's on fire is it! Now get on wi' thee, don't come that yarn, thou's not macking an April fule out of me! Gang and put it out thisell.' With that Bill slammed the window down and went back to bed.

There were always plenty of sightseers at fires, including a big gang of lads. They watched with a strange pleasure as the 'Vic' burned, and the blind owner and his family jumped to safety off the lead canopy over the front door. After, the lads stood about gaping at the activities of the firemen until well into the morning. They were very late for school and each received two strokes of the cane as a punishment.

Hubert Blades

FIRE BRIGADE PRACTICE AT RICHMOND

The town boys often went to the Fire Station in Victoria Road to watch the Brigade turn out. According to some of them 'it was better than a Charlie Chaplin film. There were constant arguments about clothes, axes or ropes . . . then someone would get another man's helmet on and there'd be chaos for a time while they changed clothes, hats and swore at one another, the place was in an uproar.'

All this went on while they were waiting for the horses to arrive to pull the Fire Engine, 'Old Emily'. The driver would be stoking the fire up, getting the boiler going ready to pump the water when they got to the fire. At that time the horses were kept in a field up behind the Barracks, that is if it was after eight o'clock at night. If the fire was later than that, the owners would have to go up to the field, a good mile walk uphill, catch the horses and bring them down for harnessing, then take them to the Fire Station. If the fire was during the sleeping hours the horsekeeper at the stables would have to be wakened – not always an easy job. The whole 'turn-out' operation could take an hour, if not longer.

Remember that the firemen – all volunteers – would be paid next to nothing for their services. What little they were paid was only for while they were actually at the fire. They still gave their services gladly!

Hubert Blades

TWO TRAVELLING SALESMEN, FORGE VALLEY

'OLD BOB' AND 'TEACAKE JOE'

The street scene was coloured by hawkers peddling their wares. There was the 'pikelet' man pushing his little cart and shouting in a high-pitched voice 'Pikelets.' These were four a penny. The 'Potman' came round with a large wicker basket balanced on his head. He walked along with a soft gait, one hand on hip, the other swinging, while we youngsters stared with admiration, possibly hoping that it would topple over to spill the miscellany of cheap mugs, jugs, pint pots, cups, saucers and plates. It never happened. The 'plant' man, carried his stock of aspidistras, castor oil plants and ferns in similar manner. . . .

Nearly every house sported an aspidistra on a fancy table near the window and the lace curtains. Some were ancient and huge with scores of rigid leaves to be washed and admired, and sired many scions for friends and relations. Pedlars, often gypsies, came with baskets of buttons, cottons, tapes and, of course, clothes pegs. If you had bought some trifle they might tell your fortune; if you didn't, they almost certainly cursed you. There were many more gypsies then than now, and Flatts Lane at Normanby was a regular camping ground and winter quarters, an added attraction to its sheltering trees being the proximity of Normanby Hall estate with splendid opportunities for their skulking lurchers.

Then, Tommy Fidler, a cripple, came round each Friday, his patient donkey pulling the gaudy hurdy-gurdy. Sometimes, a monkey was perched on the top, and what with the popular but rather tinny airs, and the antics of the monkey, he was eagerly awaited – and received, by a crowd of happy youngsters, and many not so young. Tommy had something for everybody and knew his pitch; here it would be 'Lily of Laguna,' 'Daisy Bell' or 'The shade of the old apple tree' as we sang and danced around. Further up the street there might be a little colony of ardent 'chapel-goers.' They always got 'Lead Kindly Light' at least as a final hopeful flourish. The cash which went into Tommy's tin mug determined in a degree the length of his repertoire, yet a merry lot of lads and lassies singing and jigging around, was irresistible, and he surrendered often to clamorous calls for 'Some more, Tommy – don't go yet' 'Encore' – happy days.

Then there was 'Teacake Joe' the baker. He came round with a large basket filled with cakes – stacks of tempting teacakes, buns and pastries, under each arm. And the milkmen and maids came round morning and afternoon with large cans often swinging from a shoulder yoke, dipping in their measure as required. To be sure, there were a number of local greengrocers with pony and cart hawking the streets regularly; 'Old Bob' – favourite cry 'Potatoes like balls of flour'. . .

Maurice E. Wilson

POULTERER'S SHOP, WHITBY

NANNY AND NURSERY MAID, CRATHORNE

THE TRUANT, MARY JANE

The School Attendance officer called on Wednesday and took the names of Mary Jane Alderson, Simon Alderson, Sarah Kearton and Anne Peacock. He took the name of Mary Jane Alderson, a girl over 5 years old, 10 weeks ago and though he had taken her name each of the times he has called since, she has not made one attendance.

Another boy, Wm. Peacock has not been for over a month. The Doctor gave this boy a certificate of illness some 10 weeks back and his mother is taking advantage of this certificate to keep him at home, though he is now quite well and running about the village all day long. In fact this week he has been helping one of the farmers to salve his sheep, instead of being at school. The Attendance Officer seems to do not the slightest good.

Muker School Log Book, 1 November 1889

PUNISHED FOR A ROBIN'S DROPPINGS

Another occurrence happened in which I was the culprit. It was in winter time and a robin had got into the school and was flying about; its droppings fell on to the foolscap on which I was writing. I did my best to clean it off, no doubt making a mess of it, getting it mixed up with the wet ink. When the master came round and saw my copy he was furious and gave me a clout with a book he had in his hand, this started my nose to bleed, which it was rather liable to do. However, the master told my sister to take me down to the village pump and wash my face, but on the way a relative who saw us passing took us into her house where I got a wash, but the master had seen us go in and when we returned to school he caned us for going to a relative's house.

George Harland

WHITBY

A WINTER 'BRIDE'

The nine weeks' storm of 1895 was of course the record storm. Till the great thaw came, the moorlands were covered deep with snow, which, owing to continuous frost and slight mid-day thaws, became firmly frozen over on the surface, so that one could walk without difficulty straight across country over the buried stone walls. Many houses were deep in drifts, and in one homestead the household were roused from their slumbers by hearing the sheep on the roof. The roads were continually opened by an army of farmers, only to be blocked again by recurring blizzards. The moorland sheep were brought to the lowlands, where also flocked the moorcock and all moorland birds.

In a remote ghyll lived a farmer and his housekeeper. She had been his housekeeper and mistress for twenty-three years. Often and often the moorland parson had implored him to marry her and make her an honest woman. At last he consented, and the 'spurrings' were read out for the first time on the Sunday before the great storm. Unfortunately the woman was taken seriously ill a few days afterwards. I made repeated journeys when I could to the distant farmhouse, because I was more than anxious under the circumstances to save her life. The neighbouring farmers were most sympathetic in keeping a way open for me. But alas! it was willed otherwise and our efforts were vain. To the deep sorrow of the whole ghyll she passed gently away. She was buried in her bridal dress, and her bier was dragged by hand over the great snowdrifts to the moorland church.

R.W.S. Bishop

MERITS OF THE HIRING FAIRS

Once or twice a year – in May and November – almost all the farm servants, domestic as well as outside, leave their masters' employment and have a week's holiday, repairing at such times to certain towns where 'hiring fairs' are held, in order to be re-hired by their old masters, or seek fresh employment elsewhere.

This custom certainly has its disadvantages besides its good qualities; and in the mind of a thoughtful person, I am not quite sure which would be uppermost.

With regard to the disadvantages: the system undoubtedly fosters in the majority of cases an almost total absence of what one may term a feeling of mutual interest between master and man. The agreement is only for six or twelve months, and knowing this, there is seldom that growing feeling of regard and esteem between the contracting parties that I have known to exist in cases where the arrangement is to extend indefinitely. True, there are many cases where a man will hire and re-hire himself on for many years in succession to the same master, but this is the exception rather than the rule, and should the price of labour fall, the man thus re-hired cannot but feel aggrieved at having to do the *same* work in the *same* place for a *less* wage.

The one great advantage of this mode of hiring labour is,

that should either master or man not be suited with each other, they know it is only for a time, and that the agreement will, in the due course of events, terminate at the half-year's end. The unpleasantness always attendant on 'giving notice' is thus avoided; to a sensitive-minded person, be he master or man, this is a decided advantage.

P.H. Lockwood

'NO FIXED TIME TO CEASE WORK'

In the summer time we began work about five a.m. but there was no fixed time to cease work, it was usually bedtime. The servant girl and myself milked eight cows and after feeding the stock which happened to be indoors, and other chores we would breakfast at seven a.m. This consisted of a basin of milk with a little oatmeal in it after which we had cold beef or bacon. We had coffee or tea in the same basin the milk had been in. After breakfast we went to work in the fields. Starting time in the winter was six a.m. and as all the livestock was at that time indoors there was very much more work feeding and cleaning out the houses.

George Harland

93

FEASTING THE BEES

Some of the bee customs, or what we may call bee-lore, prevalent in the district are curious. . . .

When a member of a family dies the bees must not be forgotten. Indeed, under certain circumstances connected with swarming they are thought to portend a death in the family; such for instance would be the case if they took it into their heads to swarm on the dead bough of a neighbouring tree. But when a death had actually taken place it was, and perhaps still is, no uncommon thing to put the bees into mourning. This was done by tieing a piece of black cloth or crape round the hives. But this was not all. When the funeral had taken place, and the party had returned to the house, the funeral feast began, – the *arval* as it used to be called in olden days. On these occasions the feasting was, to say the least of it, substantial. Some of the humbler classes would half ruin themselves by their lavish expenditure at these times: funeral reform had not been heard of in those days unfortunately. But what about the bees? Well! they had to be feasted also, and feasted, be it observed, in identically the same way as the house-folk had been; that is to say, a small portion gathered from every item which went to form the entertainment indoors had to be placed in a convenient situation for the bees without; such small portions were collected generally in a saucer or plate. Bread, cake, tea, sugar, beef, ham, mustard, salt; even the wine was not omitted, this being steeped into the biscuits. The idea was that if the bees were not thus feasted they would all certainly die.

Revd M.C.F. Morris

RITUAL BURIAL OF A DEAD CALF

The farms are none of them large, there not being half a dozen in the parish much over a hundred acres in extent. Nevertheless, dairies of ten or twelve cows each used to be the rule on these larger farms. And it is alleged as a fact, and by no means without reason or as contrary to experience, that if one of the cows in a dairy unfortunately produces a calf prematurely – in local phrase, 'picks her cau'f' – the remainder of the cows in the same building are only too likely, or too liable, to follow suit; of course to the serious loss of the owner. The old-world prophylactic or folklore-prescribed preventative in such a contingency used to be to remove the threshold of the cow-house in which the mischance had befallen, dig a deep hole in the place so laid bare, deep enough, indeed, to admit the abortive calf being buried in it, on its back, with its four legs all stretching vertically upwards in the rigidity of death, and then to cover all up as before.

J.C. Atkinson

WHINSTONE QUARRY WORKERS, ROSEDALE

A ROSEDALE QUARRYMAN

The path winds down to the rustic bridge at the mill. It was on the slope that the writer was once directed on his way by a countryman whose quaint figure might well have stepped out of a picture by Millet – a Rosedale quarryman it was, who had walked a long stride across the opposite moor, wearing a wide soft hat on his head, and clad in a long blue coat, and with his trousers girt about the knee, and his brown, sharp-featured, shrewd and comely face looked out from beneath the shade of a huge faggot of burnt and tangled 'ling' from the moor that he was bringing back as 'kindling' for the good wife at home. Ay, well could he remember long years ago how an ox was roasted whole on the top of the nab when 'Squire Shepherd' of Douthwaite came of age! The way to Lastingham? Ay, the 'gainest' way lay yonder. He pointed across the valley to Grouse Hall and by that way let us continue our journeying, passing over the Dove by the rustic bridge at the corn-mill, and ascending the opposite steep.

John Leyland

A WENSLEYDALE ROAD-MAKER

From Askrigg there is a road that climbs up from the end of the little street at a gradient that looks like 1 in 4, but it is really less formidable. Considering its steepness the surface is quite good, but that is due to the industry of a certain road-mender with whom I once had the privilege to talk when, hot and breathless, I paused to enjoy the great expanse that lay to the south. He was a fine Saxon type, with a sunburnt face and equally brown arms. Road-making had been his ideal when he was a mere boy, and since he had obtained his desire he told me that he couldn't be happier if he were the King of England. And his contentment seemed to me to be based largely upon his intense pleasure in bringing the roads to as great a perfection as his careful and thinking labour could compass. He did not approve of steamrollers, for his experience had taught him that if the stones were broken small enough they bound together quickly enough. Besides this, he disapproved of a great camber or curve on the road which induces the traffic to keep in the middle, leaving a mass of

SWEEP AND MILLER

loose stones on either side. The result of his work may be seen on the highway from Askrigg to Bainbridge, where a conspicuous smoothness has come to a road that was recently one of the most indifferent in the district. Perhaps he may eventually be given the maintenance of the way over the Buttertubs Pass; and if he ever induces that road to become a little more civilized, this enthusiastic workman will gain the appreciation of the whole neighbourhood. The road where we leave him, breaking every large stone he can find, goes on across a belt of brown moor, and then drops down between gaunt scars that only just leave space for the winding track to pass through. It afterwards descends rapidly by the side of a gill, and thus enters Swaledale.

Gordon Home

CHARACTERS OF HAWES

Many a story might be told of Hawes characters in the last century. There was for instance Wade the saddler; Blenkhorn, the street sweeper and dealer in turf. There was Clement Scarr, a staunch Catholic, and local adviser on Law matters – a great orator and politician to boot. This man regularly on Sundays walked from Hawes to Leyburn and back (thirty two miles) to attend service after the manner of his Faith. Another face that lingers in the memory is that of the old cobbler, with the tap-tap of his hammer on hide hard by the church gates: he to oblige his customers put many a wooden sole on to 'uppers' scarcely worth the expense. To our remarks he would answer, 'If fowks bring ma booits to clog, ah mun clog 'em.'

Edmund Bogg

THE LODGE, MALTON

DANCING IN THE KITCHEN

Music in the streets other than the Coney Street band was provided by barrel organs. There were two of them, and the owners had evidently come to some arrangement as to the days on which they could ply their trade without trespassing on each other's preserves. Each organ had its personnel of two to turn the handle, and they both came up to Clifton on different days of the week.

Having often been sent away from the front of the house they gradually learned from experience that success lay rather through an entry of the stable gates up the back lane, so they would trundle the organ into our cobbled yard and begin grinding out their wheezy tunes in front of the kitchen window.

The hour was usually between 2.30 and 3.30 in the afternoon, so, if we had come in from our walk and were preparing for lessons, we probably had a few fleeting minutes in which to enjoy ourselves.

In the kitchen the servants would be dancing in couples. In our bedroom above we were doing the same; but, as there were only three of us, one was necessarily a wallflower for part of the time.

We would throw some of our scanty hoard of pence to the men who greeted us always with smiles and grins. We never heard them speak, so they must have been foreigners, dark and swarthy-looking fellows, and we imagined that in their own country, wherever it may have been, they were assuredly brigands and desperadoes.

We used to meet less happy characters as we walked in the city. In particular there was a boy who sold papers, carried parcels to the station and sought any odd job to keep him from starvation. He was scrofulous, tubercular and dirty. He wore a thin ragged coat and trousers too short for him. He went barefoot, and he was always shivering except in the warmest weather.

His appearance did not seem to prick the conscience of any of the citizens, though people used to give him alms. He belonged to nobody. He probably slept in a doorway and never had enough to eat. We saw him growing older as we ourselves grew older.

Whenever I think of him now, he is to me the personification of Lazarus. . . .

Ethel, Lady Thomson

97

CRATHORNE HALL

UPPER-CLASS RAT CATCHERS

My mother's insistence on her social position did not prevent her from making close friends with persons who could not have found their way into Lady Londesborough's drawing-room.

One of the worst of these sub-humans was Miss Diana Pilkington, an alleged beauty.

She had a shocking influence on my mother who seemed to be entirely hypnotized by her commonness. (My mother, at that time, had but few companions. They came, but either the wind from the North Sea, or some aimless, dull, spiritual wind, blew them away again.)

On a few occasions, Miss Pilkington induced my mother to accompany her on a midnight rat-hunt in the cellars of a large hotel in Scarborough. (This was Miss Pilkington's preferred sport. But it was a strange behaviour for a woman of my mother's breeding, and fastidious cleanliness. She was, as I have said, hypnotized.)

Rat-catchers, terriers and large sticks would be collected, and Miss Pilkington would join the rat-catchers in knocking the squealing creatures on the head, and encouraging the terriers to worry their throats. Spattered with rat blood, 'the best fun in the world' she would say.

Edith Sitwell

CROQUET PLAYERS, CRATHORNE

DOMESTIC STAFF, GREAT AYTON HALL

UPSTAIRS AT LONDESBOROUGH LODGE

Lady Londesborough's footmen . . . were forbidden to look at each other in her presence, or to speak excepting in their professional capacity. They might speak to Martin, the butler, but on no account were they to look at him. Otherwise, their silence was only broken at their extreme peril.

My grandmother Londesborough never spoke to any of the servants excepting the butler Martin and the old housekeeper, Mrs. Selby, who had a face like a large red strawberry, covered with faint silvery hair. . . .

One evening, at the beginning of November, my grandmother (who was then at Londesborough Lodge in Scarborough) went up to bed with her hair of the usual brown colour. Next morning when she came down, at eleven o'clock, to an enormous breakfast (eggs and bacon, cold grouse, ham, cold partridge, home-made buns and buttercup-coloured cream and butter, hothouse peaches and grapes), the autumnal hue of her hair had changed to the most snow-bound of winters. My aunts, not daring to appear conscious of this phenomenon, stared at their plates. My grandfather concentrated on the breast of a cold partridge. The footmen seemed to be bound, more than ever, in a spell of silence.

My grandmother's white wig – for such it was – appeared at the most opportune moment, for the date was the 5th of November, a day . . . dedicated to the memory of Guy Fawkes, who had plotted to blow up the Houses of Parliament, and was then celebrated by children wheeling a perambulator containing a battered-looking dummy, and begging for 'a penny for the poor guy.'

After breakfast, on this auspicious occasion, my grandmother took up her usual place in a bathchair at the entrance of the Londesborough Lodge gardens.

Seated against a foreground of a frieze of captive daughters and a melancholy-looking footman, she must have presented a remarkable appearance. So much so that a very small curate, who was accompanied by his wife and multitudinous children, seeing her and remembering the date and its implications, placed a penny in her lap saying, genially, 'Remember, remember, the fifth of November.'

Edith Sitwell

CRATHORNE HALL, THE DRAWING ROOM

SCOTTISH FISHER GIRLS, SCARBOROUGH

WHITBY JET

An account of Whitby would not be complete without some particulars concerning 'Whitby jet.' Jet appears to be of ligneous origin, and the hard variety, which is the true 'Whitby jet,' occurs in thin bands, worked with great and increasing difficulty. It has a fine texture, is unaffected by temperature, is durable, takes a high polish, and lends itself to delicate manipulation. The scarcity of the hard jet has led to the importation of a hard Spanish variety of somewhat inferior quality, which is wrought at Whitby, and seems to stand midway between the best native kind and the soft Whitby jet, which is cheap and effective when new, but soon loses its polish or breaks. The use of the material for the making of ornaments is of high antiquity, for it occurs in the houes or burial-mounds of Cleveland, and, from discoveries of jet objects in the neighbourhood of the abbey, it was clearly prized in the Middle Ages. . . .

The modern growth of the industry dates from the beginning of this century, when much encouragement was given to the workers, and is greatly due to the introduction of jet at court; but, through change of fashion, and perhaps through the indiscriminate use of the soft kind of jet in past times, the industry is now somewhat depressed, though a period of court morning will usually give activity to it again.

John Leyland

WHITBY JET IN SAN FRANCISCO

The '*San Francisco Daily News*' in a recent issue says 'Mrs. James B. Duke leads American women of social prominence in following a fashion inaugurated by Queen Alexandra in the wearing of necklaces of jet. Mrs. Duke's beads are said to be the prettiest in America, the beads at the back increasing in size until at the throat they are as large as hazel nuts. They are of the famous Whitby Jet and have been given a wonderful finish, almost velvety to the touch, by a new and secret process. Mrs. Duke is wearing them in preference to the 200,000 dollar pearl necklace given by her husband.'

Whitby Gazette, 13 December 1907

THE WHITBY FISHERMAN

He is of medium height, rather stout, rough-looking with shaggy eyebrows, weather-beaten face, keen eyes despite his many years, and old-fashioned clothes. He is much in request. His many pockets contain stray pennies, small packets of sweets and many other things may be found therein, therefore the children love him. He is careful yet generous, large-hearted, keen-witted, not much of a scholar, but a positive hero of the sea. He is a man who says very little, unless appealed to, and keeps his breath to cool his porridge, or that he may have it when putting out to sea.

W.B. Pickering

WHITBY FISHERMEN

NURSING STAFF, PICKERING

A 'MOST GLORIOUS REMUNER'

Another aspect of life in practice was the large number of grateful patients, who not only paid their bills with satisfaction but also sent very handsome presents; and one of these gifts had been accompanied by a note saying, 'We hope Dr. English will accept the enclosed as a small remuneration for his great skill and kindness.' I, being fond of words, seized 'remuneration' (new to my vocabulary) with delight, and began to use it on every possible occasion. My Father joined me in this sport, and from that time onwards referred to all his presents as remunerations; till the word became a family joke, and was affectionately shortened to 'remuner'. . . .

But one remuner will never be forgotten; a remuner so astounding that we could scarce believe our eyes: a remuner to end all silver hot water jugs, gold watches, diamond rings, and sets of pewter dish covers: a real live remuner: in fact a cow! Thomas himself was, for the moment, quite overcome on seeing it; and, when the animal had been led into the yard, he could hardly express his thanks sufficiently. For the value of a cow, or 'Coo price', was synonymous with untold riches, and how could he possibly have earned so much gratitude? There was no answering such rhetoric, and the cow went down to posterity as the most glorious remuner of all time!

Brenda H. English

SURGERY IN THE KITCHEN

As only three surgical beds were available at the Whitby Cottage Hospital, my Father usually carried out operations at the houses of his patients, and on these occasions my Mother generally accompanied him. The folding operating table was then set up in front of the kitchen fire, the instruments placed in lysol, and cotton wool swabs in a bowl of boiled water. Thomas would administer chloroform, then rush round the table and operate at top speed, till the patient began to show signs of coming round, when he would either prolong the anaesthetic or stitch up the wound, according to the stage reached. Almost all emergencies and major operations were carried out in this way, strangely enough usually with satisfactory results, though medical readers will note the absence of aseptic precautions. Yet one must remember that Thomas and Louie had only just emerged from the London Hospital, where carbolic sprays and sponges had been the order of the day, while gloves were not yet tolerated by many surgeons since these, being much too thick when first introduced, impeded their dexterity.

Brenda H. English

CHURCH ARMY CARAVAN, SWAINBY

'T'LAST OOT PUTS T'BUSH IT HOLE'

The church [at Lunds] is a primitive barn-like building, and on our first visit some fourteen years ago, was in sad disrepair, but it has now been renovated. Barker, author of the 'Three Days in Wensleydale', relates that he once attended service in this chapel in winter, when the seats and floor were covered with snow to a depth of two or three inches. One story has it that for many years the church was minus a door, so, to prevent cattle finding shelter within the sanctuary, a big thorn bush was thrust securely into the doorway, and the unwritten law of the church-going dalesman was, 'T'last oot puts t'bush it hole.' To this lonesome wind and rain-swept God's acre, the dead were borne over the high moor from Cotterdale for burial. The old track which crosses high Abbotside and thence down to Lunds Church is still known as the 'corpse road'. Here, too, sleeps that original character, an itinerant pedlar of small wares for women-folk, whose far and wide soubriquet was 'Thread Jack'. A parson's farewell address to his congregation on leaving this church was, 'You do not love one another, and God does not love you: for in all these three or four years I have ministered here, there has not been a marriage or a death.'

Edmund Bogg

DIAMOND WEDDING, WEST AYTON

VILLAGE DOCTOR, NORTON

'MY LADY TONGUE'

Our local medico was visiting an old lady, an old acquaintance of mine, who always had 'a gert gude dish' of 'my Lady Tongue' ready for instant production. She was in peril of her life with haemorrhage, which the doctor had had much difficulty in staying, and which might come on again at any moment, and was almost safe to recur if she began her usual voluble chatter. However, talk she would, and at last the doctor, out of patience with her, addressed her sharply in her own tongue: 'Ho'd thah noise, thee blethering au'd feeal, or Ah'll tie thah toongue ti thah teeath;' the instantaneous rejoinder being, 'Thee caan't, doctor; fur Ah ha'e na a teeath i' mah heead!' But much of this readiness seems a thing of the past now, and I think it is because the stiffness of the 'New English' instilled in the Elementary School lends itself both less familiarly and less well to the ready expression of quaint conceit or incisive repartee.

As further illustrative in the same connection, I may perhaps mention the following. Making inquiry one day about a person who, I had supposed, was no longer single, I was answered as follows: 'Neea, neea, he's nane married. He still trails a leeght harrow: his hat covers his household.' And from an old note-book I extract the next: 'He's ower mickle a feeal to ken how many beans mak's five.' Of a miserly skinflint, 'He wad skin tweea deevils for yah pelt.' Of an emaciated man, 'He's that thin, he's lahk a ha'porth o' soap efter a lang day's weshing.' Of a woman newly but not wisely married, 'Ay, she's tied a knot with her tongue she'll be matched to unloose wiv her teeath.' And lastly this, of a man without brains or 'gumption,' 'Ay, there's t'heead an' t'hair; but there's nowght else.'

J.C. Atkinson

NO SILLY MODESTY ABOUT THEIR BODIES

I found the families of the county squires incomparably the most agreeable and satisfactory patients to attend. Once their confidence gained, they were the most loyal and considerate of friends and supporters.

One great drawback in attending at the large houses was the valuable time lost in running the gauntlet of so many flunkeys. Attending a great lady, I was conducted from the front door to the library by a footman, from the library to Miladi's boudoir by the butler, from the boudoir to a dressing-room by her maid, and from the latter to the sick-room by the nurse. Time twenty minutes. The next morning I walked up unannounced to Miladi's bedroom and knocked at the door.

'Who is there?' asked Miladi.

'The doctor,' I answered.

'Oh I'm not ready,' she protested, but I told her I was anxious to see her when she was not ready, so that I could more easily judge of her true condition. This making of the patient ready and pretty by fastidious nurses is often very deceptive. I remember well a case where a specialist saw a patient who, after being made ready and pretty, pulled himself together in extraordinary fashion although desperately ill. To our astonishment the great man gave a most favourable prognosis, only to have the mortification after lunch of reversing it. The patient died the next day.

The gentlefolk had nothing of the silly modesty about the functions of their bodies, which is so evident among the middle classes. Many of the latter would lower their voices to a whisper and look so very mysterious that one might think some momentous secret was on the point of revelation.

R.W.S. Bishop

INN AT SCARBOROUGH

''IGH, 'AUGHTY, AND POMPEY'

I shall not easily forget my first professional visit to a Yorkshire dale. Being a Yorkshireman I knew quite well that unless I wished to earn a reputation of being ''igh, 'aughty, and pompey,' I must accept on a first visit any hospitality offered me. At the first farmhouse after my consultation was over, I was asked by the farmer, 'What will ye tak?' Thinking a little whisky would be the least injurious under the circumstances, I asked for it. The housewife's face became at once solemn and serious and as long as a fiddle before she said, 'Ye are welcome reight eneagh to t'drop o' whisky, but we deean't want any mair drunken doctors in t'shop.' What a stupid blunder on my part. Then I went on to the next farmhouse where I was also asked what I would 'tak.' 'A glass of milk,' I replied, with great self-confidence. But the second housewife's face became, if possible, even more serious and solemn than the previous one's. 'Ye are welcome,' she explained, 'to t'drop o' milk, but we deean't want any mair drunken doctors. Dr Macpherson, when he fust came, used to axe for milk like ye, and thens he axed for whisky which war his ruin.' I had escaped from Scylla to Charybdis, and it was all very perplexing. I was informed afterwards that the majority of my predecessors had been topers and 'drunken dogs.'

R.W.S. Bishop

A CAREFUL DRINKER

A stranger on a walking tour called at a Yorkshire moorland inn for a refreshing drink. The only other occupant of the bar was a cattle drover, and in a high good humour he asked the latter if he would have a glass of ale. 'Aye, thankee,' was the reply, and he immediately swallowed the glassful which had been drawn for him in one 'let down.' 'Will you have another?' asked the kindly stranger. 'Thankee ageean,' responded the drover, and as promptly swallowed the second glass at one gulp. 'Have a third?' offered the stranger, in deep admiration. The third glassful was again promptly 'necked' at one asking. Quoth the stranger, 'You must be very thirsty.' 'Noa, Noa,' protested the drover. 'Yeah seea,' very confidentially, 'yance Ah had yan knocked ower.'

R.W.S. Bishop

106

WHITBY POLICE FOOTBALL TEAM

TRAINING THE POLICE

On appointment to the Force, recruits were drilled by the drill instructor for three or four hours a day. The remainder of the time was spent by recruits in the Guard Room (now called the Charge Room), where they apparently picked up from the older Constables all they needed to know about the work of a policeman, or at least, enough to enable them to take their places on the beat. Neither legal training nor any general instruction as to the performance of their duties was given; however, before being sent to a division the recruits were interviewed by the Chief Constable, who gave them a talk on the conduct expected of them when they reached their stations. Among other things, they were told that if they wanted a drink while on duty, they could go into a public house and get one, provided they paid for it, did not stay too long to drink it, did not drink to excess, and did not stay drinking with the general public. (This could easily have been the cause of so many policemen getting drunk on duty in those days.)

On being posted to South Bank, P.C. Clark reported to Inspector Dowsland, whose first two questions were, 'Where have you come from?' and 'Can you fight?' There was much drunkenness at South Bank, with the consequent high number of street brawls and assaults on the Police. Public houses were open from 6 a.m. to 11 p.m. on weekdays, and a man could get down to some really serious drinking. P.C. Clark's fighting talents were soon even further improved.

Maurice E. Wilson

PRISON FOR STEALING A TURNIP

An ill-clad, half-starved man, named Goonricke, was charged at Scarborough with the theft of a turnip. When the farmer accosted him he was hungrily eating half of the turnip, and carrying the other half under his arm. He pleaded to the North Riding magistrates that he took the turnip because he was very hungry, but the Bench ordered him to pay 7s 6d or go to gaol for a week. Goonricke asked for time to pay, but this was refused. It was the man's first appearance before the Court. He was at one time a prosperous tradesman in Scarborough.

The Teesdale Mercury, 18 November 1903

AN INDULGENT MAGISTRATE

Some of the old squires I knew were quite proud of their old Yorkshire, and often talked it as broadly as possible in addressing the herd. One, a baronet, who unfortunately drank heavily, and was often carried to bed in a helpless state by one of my friends, was chairman of the bench of magistrates in his district, but for a long time had dealt out justice in a ridiculously lenient fashion, carrying matters with a very high hand. At last his brother magistrates, tired of being ignored, held an indignation meeting, threatening to report him to the Lord Chancellor unless he mended his ways. He was very contrite, promising immediate amendment, but at the very next case which came before him, completely forgot his

THE SCOTS GREYS LEAVE KIRBYMOORSIDE

promise. It was a double one of assault and drunkenness. He thus pronounced sentence to the offending Yorkshire man. 'Noo thens, for t'assault we'll fine yer a shilling and costs. As for t'drunkenness we'll say nowt about it, as we get drunk oorsells.'

R.W.S. Bishop

NORTH YORK MILITIA IN TRAINING

In 1889 and 1900 training again took place on Richmond racecourse. In the latter of those years, Lieutenant Basil Hood, then of the Yorkshire Regiment, afterwards well known as the author of '*Merrie England*' and other musical comedies, acted as instructor of musketry, and in that capacity succeeded in raising the figure of merit in the battalion.

Robert Bell Turton

'ONE LOVELY DAY IN LATE SUMMER'

One lovely day in late Summer when the bracken on our hills was just beginning to go rusty, and the swallows were starting to muster, the strains of marching music and the tramp of marching men, came down the road; men in khaki with rifles at the slope, smart and proud, some with faces set and grim, some devil-may-care. A sharp command, a stamping halt, and a brief release while wives and children, sweethearts and friends, kissed, shook hands, and said Good-bye! The band struck up:

> Farewell, farewell – my own true home,
> I cannot bear to leave you . . .
> I go where duty calls me . . .

and tears trickled and flowed, and people waved and shouted, and the train moved off with khaki filling every door and window, and Bob Storey's fog signals along the line popped in succession as the engine pulled away and 'D' Coy. of the 4th Yorks. Territorial Battalion went off to war on that lovely late Summer day in 1914.

Maurice E. Wilson

YORK STATION

CONVENIENCE OF A SEASON TICKET

It may be added that the North Eastern have marched in the van of most railways in the kingdom in affording facilities for the exploration of the country. In addition to ordinary tourist tickets, thousand-mile tickets, and similar conveniences, they have established a very complete system of circular tours. In particular, they have recently initiated a scheme which might well be imitated by other lines – the issue of sectional season tickets for a week or other short period. The convenience of this is immense, – the visitor, for instance, who is staying in *Wensleydale* can thus travel up and down the valley for the week as often as he pleases at the cost of a very few shillings.

J.E. Morris

'A GENTLEMAN AMONG STATIONS'

Outside the weather-beaten walls [of York], in which 'the moss is weaving its tapestry,' there is to-day a dash of another sort . . . the dash of the locomotive. The great station, with its bold sweep of main line and ample sidings, accommodates more than two hundred trains daily, from the 'Flying Scotsman' to the humblest stopper that crawls out Seamer way 'to watch the corn grow.' There is no station more interesting than that of York. With its handsome hotel, it is a gentleman among stations. It seems almost to take its proportions from the grand old minster close by. It is lofty and spacious; handsome so far as a railway station can be, and attractive from its brightness, its light lines, and the harmoniousness of its colouring. A modern novelist has made a picture of life at York Station the appropriate opening to his interesting story; and certainly there is no platform that affords more scope for the student of character. There is a flavour of London about the group of business men who have come down by the East Coast express, and are taking their five-course dinner in the refreshment-room; but there is little of the intense hurry, or of the grind of town, in evidence here. There is a crowd at the refreshment-counter, another by the bookstall, and a shoal of people on the long, curving platform. But they are altogether different in stamp from the surging crowd that rushes to catch the morning train into the City.

The stately dignity of York is alien to hurry; if it hurries at

109

STATION STAFF, POTTO

all, its quickened step and bustle are associated rather with pleasure than with trade. In summer and autumn it is the halting-place of a multitude, full of the anticipation of enjoyment, on their way to the seaside – to Scarborough with its spa and music, to Filey with its spray-flecked brig and sea-bird colony of Speeton, and to Bridlington with its fine old harbour and new promenade and boating paradise. Later it is thronged with hunting-men, and there is the rattle of horse-boxes in the sidings. At Convocation the platform is crowded with bishops and clergy; and it was at one time a fine sight to see the great, manly form of Archbishop Thomson, moving giant-like among the crowd, and to hear his deep-voiced welcome, hearty and sincere even to his foe, Canon Body, and even to the Bishop of Ripon, the only member of the Upper House who has dared to shock ecclesiastical susceptibilities by discarding the knee-breeches and gaiters of the prelate and donning a pair of broadcloth trousers!

John Pendleton

THE 'MISSING LINK' RAILWAY

The Scarboro' and Whitby had been pronounced to be a very important and interesting line. It supplies the 'missing link' of coast railway communications between the Tweed and the Humber. It will bring about the development of a district, hitherto almost unexplored, replete with scenic attractions and valuable natural productions. The Scarboro' and Whitby Railway will probably come into most distinct prominence and popularity as an excursion and pleasure traffic railway. It will be *par excellence* 'The Visitors Line'.

The new coast railway is only some 20 miles in length. The accustomed route from Whitby to Scarboro', via Pickering, is more than 40 miles long, so that a substantial saving both in time and money will be realised by the travelling public, who may congratulate themselves on the economic improvement effected for them. Many thousands of visitors will doubtless avail themselves of it every season.

Starting from West Cliff Station at Whitby, the river Esk is crossed by means of a splendid viaduct, an exceedingly well built structure and a noble example of engineering skill and science. After passing Hawsker, the next station reached is Robin Hood's Bay, a quaint and ancient fishing town. . . .

Robin Hood's Bay is already bestirring itself, and promises to become a most popular and attractive sanatorium and health resort on the Yorkshire coast, the fresh breezes being (so medical authorites say) impregnated with the finest ozone. There is excellent bathing to be had at no great distance on the sands, and bathing machines have already made their appearance, to the astonishment of the simple natives, who wonder what things are coming to, for it is a primitive community, and the good folks are as yet unsophisticated. The homely, old-fashioned, and unpretending houses are already engaged by visitors for the season at liberal figures, and the fortune of the whole place seems to be on the way of being made. The railway station is very conveniently placed, and, if the railway does nothing else it will add one more to the number of our fashionable Yorkshire watering places.

Whitby Times, 18 July 1885

ROBIN HOOD'S BAY WORTHIES

ROBIN HOOD'S BAY

Robin Hood's Bay town is unique amongst English fishing villages, and whenever one visits it one feels constrained to wish that nobody had ever discovered it but one's self. Since it was discovered the enterprising builder has been at work, and between it and Fylingthorpe has built a number of modern houses, villas and bungalows (so-called), at which no one should look as he makes his way down to the quaint and queer little cluster of cottages lying between two sister cliffs at the foot of the headlands. No one surely ever saw quite such a strangely built place as this! It is scarcely exaggeration to say that you can step off the threshold of one house on the roof of another, or look out of your own window down your neighbour's chimney: it is certainly none to say that a good many houses were built so close upon the edge of the cliffs that they eventually fell over them. It is also recorded that upon one occasion a vessel being driven ashore poked its bowsprit into the window of the inn – an accident which might very easily occur again. A delightfully picturesque, quaint place this, and whether it ever was connected with that mysterious outlaw Robin Hood or not, it is a place wherein lovers of the ancient things, of the smell of the sea, and of stories thereof told by brown-faced gentlemen in blue jerseys, whose eyes are perpetually on the look-out, will enjoy quietude and beautiful air to their hearts' content.

J.S. Fletcher

A VISIT TO STAITHES

Scarcely two miles from Hinderwell is the fishing-hamlet of Staithes, wedged into the side of a deep and exceedingly picturesque beck. Here – and it is the same at Runswick – one is obliged to walk warily during the painter's season, for fear of either obstructing the view of the man behind the easel you have just passed, or out of regard for the feelings of some girls just in front. There are often no more chances of standing still in Staithes than may be enjoyed on a popular golf-links on a fine Saturday afternoon. These folk at Staithes do not disturb one with cries of 'Fore!' but with that blank Chinaman's stare which comes to anyone who paints in public.

The average artist is a being who is quite unable to recognise architectural merit. He sees everything to please him if the background of his group be sufficiently tumble-down and derelict. If this be incorrect, how could such swarms of artistic folk paint and actually lodge in Staithes? The steep road leading past the station drops down into the village, giving a glimpse of the beck crossed by its ramshackle wooden foot-bridge – the view one has been prepared for by guide-books and picture postcards. Lower down you enter the village street. Here the smell of fish comes out to greet you, and one would forgive the place this overflowing welcome if one were not so shocked at the dismal aspect of the houses on either side of the way. Many are of comparatively recent origin, others are quite new, and a few – a very few – are old; but none have any architectural pretensions or any claims to picturesqueness, and

STAITHES AND ITS FOLK

only a few have the neat and respectable look one is accustomed to expect after seeing Robin Hood's Bay.

Staithes had filled me with so much pleasant expectancy that my first walk down this street of dirty, ugly houses had brought me into a querulous frame of mind, and I wondered irritably why the women should all wear lilac-coloured bonnets, when a choice of colour is not difficult as far as calico is concerned. Those women who were in mourning had dyed theirs black, and these assorted well with the colour of the stone of many of the houses.

I hurried down on to the little fish-wharf – a wooden structure facing the sea – hoping to find something more cheering in the view of the little bay, with its bold cliffs, and the busy scene where the cobles were drawn up on the shingle. Here my spirits revived, and I began to find excuses for the painters. The little wharf, in a bad state of repair, like most things in the place, was occupied by groups of stalwart fisher-folk, men and women.

The men were for the most part watching their women-folk at work. They were also to an astonishing extent mere spectators in the arduous work of hauling the cobles one by one on to the steep bank of shingle. A tackle hooked to one of the balks of timber forming the staith was being hauled at by

five women and two men! Two others were in a listless fashion leaning their shoulders against the boat itself. With the last 'Heave-ho!' at the shortened tackle the women laid hold of the nets, and with casual male assistance laid them out on the shingle, removed any fragments of fish, and generally prepared them for stowing in the boat again.

It is evidently an accepted state of things at Staithes that the work of putting out to sea and the actual catching of the fish is sufficient for the men-folk, for the feminine population do their arduous tasks with a methodical matter-of-factness which surprises only the stranger. I was particularly struck on one occasion with the sight of a good-looking and very neatly dressed young fishwife who was engaged in that very necessary but exceedingly unpleasant task of cutting open fish and removing the perishable portions. With unerring precision the sharp knife was plunged into each cod or haddock, and the fish was in its marketable condition in shorter time than one can write. A little boy plunged them into a pail of ruddy-looking water, and from thence into the regulation fish box or basket that finds its way to the Metropolis.

Gordon Home

112

THREE WRECKS AT SCARBOROUGH

'A PERFECTLY HORRIBLE SUPERSTITION'

A perfectly horrible superstition still remains to be mentioned.
It was considered unlucky to save a drowning man. . . .

Whether or not this arose from the isolation of these coast
places, and the fear lest the food stored up for the winter
would not hold out if there were many more mouths to feed,
or whether it was that vessels could be more safely plundered
if there were no survivors to tell the tale, certain it is that the
fishermen had a superstitious dread of saving a stranger, lest by
an evil eye or magical charm, he should be able to do them an
injury. The old people could tell tales of men nearly dragged
ashore, and then, by the advice of the elders, abandoned to
their fate lest ill-fortune should result from saving them.

Revd A.N. Cooper

STORM AT SANDSEND

113

A PLEASANT EVENING AT SANDSEND

We spent the night at the Beach Hotel, Sandsend, where, in the coffee-room, we met some pleasant people from London, who had been led so far north by the A.B.C. Guide. We stayed up till midnight discussing the peculiarities of the Yorkshire and Lancashire character, and while we talked, ever and anon the waves threw their spray on the windows of the room in which we were sitting. The people of the house told us that sometimes in the winter the waves actually dash right over the house and fill the rain-tubs at the back with salt-water. Every one to their taste; but I shouldn't care to live in a house where there was a chance of being washed out of bed some night.

Revd H. Wild

ORIGINAL POETRY ON THE YEAR OF OUR LORD, 1895

> But October came with wind and hail,
> And lofty ships could hardly sail.
> For while they were on the ocean tossed
> I heard that many a life was lost.
>
> When November came it was much the same,
> It was not snow but fell much rain,
> The nights were dark, the wind was strong,
> It was a struggle to get along;
> For a man who had to cross the moor
> He had a task we may be sure,
> I was told that he did lose his way,
> And had to wait till the break of day;

> He could not there resort to wire,
> But with some turf he made a fire,
> And behind a butt he sat him down,
> For he was far from either friend or town;
> And as he sat upon a stone
> He thought of them who were at home;
> When morning came he tried again,
> And urged his way with might and main;
> The road he travelled he did not ken,
> But he landed at Hardle just at ten,
> And while to them he told his story,
> The friends for him were very sorry;
> They said he was neither mean nor shabby,
> But he wanted to be to Rosedale Abbey!
>
> December came to close the year,
> On every side there was much cheer,
> And all around there was such mirth
> It reminded us of the Saviour's birth,
> For as shepherds watched their flocks by night
> They were guided by a star so bright;
> And angels did so sweetly sing
> Which told they did good tidings bring.
> So now let all unite and sing
> A song of praise to Christ our King,
> That when our race on earth is run
> The Lord at last may say well done.
> My poem now it must be ended,
> I have said much more than I intended,
> And there's many a thing that must be done
> But the harvest's past, the year is gone.

John Magginson

Sources & Photographic Details

TEXT

The page numbers given below relate to pages in this book and not the page numbers of the source books.

The main sources for descriptive text are: Canon J.C. Atkinson *Forty Years in a Moorland Parish*, pp. 14, 15, 16, 19, 20, 25, 28, 29, 30, 53, 58, 66, 81, 94, 105; Dr R.W.S. Bishop *My Moorland Patients* pp. 11, 17, 21, 24, 34, 38, 42, 51, 52, 82, 92, 105, 106, 107; Richard Blakeborough *Yorkshire: Wit, Character and Folklore* pp. 11, 19, 21, 31, 32, 45, 65, 66, 67, 68, 75, 85, 86; Edmund Bogg *Wild Borderland of Richmondshire* pp. 18, 27, 28, 30, 39, 41, 53, 55, 57, 69, 70, 74, 86, 96, 104.

Other works used are: Lady Bell *At the Works* p. 47; Hubert Blades and Julia Ghent *Remembering Richmond* p. 88; Revd A.N. Cooper *Across the Broad Acres* pp. 36, 50, 60, 113; Brenda H. English *Five Generations of a Whitby Medical Family* pp. 71, 103; J. Fairfax-Blakeborough *Yorkshire Village Life, Humour and Characters* p. 36, *Malton Memories and L'Anson Triumphs* p. 77; J.S. Fletcher *The Enchanting North* p. 111; Joseph Ford *Reminiscences* p. 51; George Harland *Queen of the Dales* pp. 31, 40, 41, 63, 64, 80, 91, 93; Michael Heavisides *Walks around Cleveland* p. 69; Gordon Home *Yorkshire Dales and Fells* pp. 37, 59, 65, 73, 95, 111; Storm Jameson *Journey from the North* p. 43; Charles Knightly (ed.) *Country Voices* pp. 11, 13, 39, 43, 47, 54, 58, 82; Tom Laughton *Pavilions by the Sea* pp. 83, 84; John Leyland *The Yorkshire Coast* pp. 95, 101; P.H. Lockwood *Storm and Sunshine in the Dales* pp. 9, 93; Thomas and Catherine Macquaid *About Yorkshire* pp. 60, 61; C.T. Maltby *Yorkshire for Me* p. 9; J.E. Morris *North Riding of Yorkshire* pp. 23, 52, 109; Revd M.C.F. Morris *Yorkshire Folk Talk* pp. 85, 94; John Pendleton *Our Railways* p. 109; Herbert Read *The Innocent Eye* pp. 20, 22; Frank H. Reynard *The Bedale Hounds 1832–1908* p. 78; B. Seebohm Rowntree *Poverty: a Study of Town Life* pp. 13, 48; Edith Sitwell *Taken Care of* pp. 25, 98, 99; J. Sutcliffe Smith *Music of the Yorkshire Dales* p. 55; Mrs Rodolph Stawell *Motor Tours in Yorkshire* p. 23; Ethel, Lady Thomson *Clifton Lodge* pp. 49, 62, 74, 97; Two Sunday School Teachers *Holiday Rambles on the Yorkshire Moors* pp. 18, 46, 61; Leslie Wenham (ed.) *History of Richmond School* pp. 14, 73, 75; Revd H. Wild *Holiday Walks in the North-Countree* p. 114; Maurice E. Wilson *The Story of Eston* pp. 51, 79, 89, 107, 108.

Newspapers include: the *Richmond Chronicle* p. 42; the *Teesdale Mercury* p. 107; the *Whitby Gazette* pp. 33, 34, 101; and the *Whitby Times* p. 110.

ILLUSTRATIONS

The credits and information on all of the illustrations used in this book are given in page ascending order. Where a source is referred to frequently, only initials are used, and a key to these is given at the end of this section. Where dates are known, or can reasonably accurately be deduced, these are given.

Front endpapers: Yarm Cycling Club, *c.* 1905 (MR); half-title page, A conservatory of Scarborough; title page, Cycling party, Catterick, *c.* 1910 (DG); page 1, Great Ayton Brass Band, 1879 (DOS); page 2, Cricket festival, Hutton-le-Hole, *c.* 1910 (RFM); page 3, Election campaign, Scarborough, 1911 (WS); page 4, Herbert Summerson, *c.* 1895 (DG); page 5, Cart and carriage, Scarborough (WS); page 6, Market Place, Scarborough (WS); page 7, Guisborough Family, *c.* 1890 (DG); page 9, Shooting party, Swainby (RC); page 10, Yarm Angling Association, 1909 (MR); Old Peter the gamekeeper, Swainby (RC); page 11, Children's Corner, Scarborough, 1890s (RC); page 12, Crab Wheel, Sutton, *c.* 1895 (DG); page 13, Golden Jubilee Feast, Great Ayton, 1897 (DOS); page 14, Market Place, Leyburn, *c.* 1900 (RC); page 15, Swainby from the bridge, 1905 (RC); page 16, Wheelgate, Malton, *c.* 1910 (DG); page 17, Old Scarborough Harbour, 1880s (Scarborough Public Library); page 18, Brompton, 1905 (DG); page 19, Concert party, Scarborough, *c.* 1912 (WS); page 20, Sandsend from Lythe Bank, *c.* 1890 (DG); page 21, West Ayton, *c.* 1890 (LS); Two sisters, West Ayton, *c.* 1895 (LS); page 23, Buttertubs Pass, Swaledale, 1908 (DG); page 24, Ravenscar Station, 1901 (RC); page 25, Scarborough Beach, 1890s (WS); page 26, Scarborough poster, 1900 (National Railway Museum, York); page 27, The *Fearless* at Scarborough, 1885 (WS); page 28, Cayton village, 1910 (DG); page 29, The rector leaves Yarm church, 1904 (MR); page 30, Market Place, Hawes, 1896 (DG); page 31, On the shore, Scarborough, *c.* 1910 (RC); page 32, Boer War veterans return to Yarm, 1902 (MR); page 33, Coronation Day, Whitby, 1911 (Whitby Literary and Philosophical Society); Old Market Place, Whitby, 1884 (DG); page 34, Coronation celebrations, Helmsley, 1903 (RFM); page 35, Talbot Inn, Scarborough, 1902 (WS); page 36, The Farmer's Inn, Scorton, 1892 (RC); page 37, The post office, Terrington, 1888 (DG); William Raine, postmaster, West Ayton, *c.* 1905 (LS); page 38, Maynard's Bridge, Swainby, *c.* 1900 (RC); page 39, Fishing fleet, Scarborough, *c.* 1880 (Scarborough Public Library); page 40, Danby Lodge, 1890s (DG); page 41, Mowing bracken, Ferndale *c.* 1905 (RFM); page 42, Thatched haystacks, Skiplay

Grange, *c.* 1902 (RFM); page 43, The Noted Chocolate Stores, Forge Valley, early 1900s (LS); page 44, Old Cottage and beck, Helmsley, *c.* 1885 (DG); Family portrait, Middlesbrough (T. Bainbridge); page 45, The Demaine sisters, Kearton, 1888 (Mrs M. Holmes); page 46, Stepping stones at Hutton-le-Hole, *c.* 1912 (RFM); page 47, Tannery workers, Aislaby, 1890s (MR); page 48, Middlesbrough, *c.* 1895 (RC); page 49, Swainby Brass Band, 1890s (RC); page 50, Bird's egg collectors, Ravenscar, 1883 (WS); page 51, Market day, Northallerton, *c.* 1905 (RC); page 52, Market Place, Pickering, 1890s (RC); page 53, Wedding at Battersby Junction, 1903 (DG); page 54, Church parade, West Ayton, 1904 (LS); Revd James Alder Wilson, rector of Crathorne, 1902 (MO); page 55, Ox cart, Helmsley (RC); page 56, Village band, Keld, *c.* 1898 (Alec and Margaret Baines); page 57, Levisham Valley, *c.* 1905 (DG); page 58, Bolton Castle, 1890s (DG); page 59, Unloading coal from the *Diamond* (FMS); page 60, Runswick Bay, 1895 (FMS); page 61, *Dunrobin* stranded at Seaton, 1896 (WS); page 62, Beckhole, Goathland, 1890s (DG); page 63, Rustic idyll (FMS); page 64, East Ayton School, 1900 (LS); page 65, The Seamer Express, *c.* 1905 (LS); page 66, Ellerby, *c.* 1893 (DG); page 67, Salton Green, 1909 (DG); Master Summerson, Saltburn, 1882 (DG); page 68, Display of toys at Middlesbrough School, 1904 (T. Bainbridge); Village schoolmaster, Runswick, 1901 (DG); page 69, Somewhere in Ryedale (RFM); page 70, Thwaite, *c.* 1908 (DG); page 71, Excursion to the Forge Valley (National Railway Museum); Staintondale, 1901 (DG); page 72, The Dobson brothers, Yarm, *c.* 1907 (MR); page 73, Richmond, 1902 (DG); page 74, Waterfall and church, Thornton-le-Dale, 1905 (DG); page 75, School party at Leyburn, 1912 (Haxby Road School, York); page 76, Headmaster, family and his staff, Great Ayton, *c.* 1905 (DOS); page 77, Foxton's Livery Stables, Scarborough, 1906 (WS); page 78, The Zetland Meet at Middleton Lodge (DG); page 79, At the smithy, Ryedale (RFM); page 80, The village store, Lastingham, 1890s (RFM); page 81, Crosby's Mansion, Hutton Buscel, *c.* 1905 (LS); page 82, Swainby meeting (RC); page 83, South Bay, Scarborough (J. Robin Lidster collection); page 84, Scarborough Beach, 1890s (WS); Fresh oysters, Scarborough (WS); page 85, Rotunda Museum, Scarborough (Rotunda Museum, Scarborough); page 86, Pickering, *c.* 1900 (WS); page 87, Floods at York, October 1892 (DG); Fire at Victoria Hotel, Richmond, 1908 (Audrey Carr); page 88, Richmond Castle and bridge, *c.* 1900 (DG); page 89, Two travelling salesmen, *c.* 1905 (LS); page 90, Poulterers shop, Whitby (FMS); page 91, Nanny and nursery maid, Crathorne, *c.* 1890 (MO); page 92, Whitby (FMS); page 93, Society of Shepherds, Helmsley, *c.* 1894 (RFM); page 94, Staindale, 1895 (WS); page 95, Whinstone Quarry workers, Rosedale (DOS); page 96, Sweep and miller (FMS); page 97, The Lodge, Malton, 1902 (DG); page 98, Crathorne Hall, *c.* 1910 (MO); Croquet players, Crathorne (MO); page 99, Domestic staff, Great Ayton Hall (DOS); page 100, Crathorne Hall, the drawing room (MO); page 101, Scottish fisher girls, Scarborough, 1890s (DG); page 102, Whitby fishermen (FMS); page 103, Nursing staff, Pickering, 1905 (LS); page 104, Church Army caravan, Swainby (RC); Diamond Wedding, West Ayton, 1903 (LS); page 105, Village doctor, Norton, *c.* 1895 (DG); page 106, Inn at Scarborough (WS); page 107, Whitby Police Football Team (Whitby Literary and Philosophical Society); page 108, The Scots Greys leave Kirkbymoorside, 1914 (RFM); page 109, York Station, 1890s (National Railway Museum, York); page 110, Station staff, Potto (RC); page 111, Robin Hood's Bay worthies (RC); page 112, Staithes and its women, *c.* 1886 (DG); page 113, Three wrecks at Scarborough, 1891 (WS); Storm at Sandsend, 1903 (DG); page 114, Launch of Scarborough Lifeboat, 1893 (WS); back endpapers, Yarm Cycling Club picnic at Stone Mill, 1906 (MR).

Key: DG, Author's collection; DOS, Dan O'Sullivan, Great Ayton; FMS, photographs taken by Frank Meadow Sutcliffe, Sutcliffe Gallery, Whitby; LS, Lilian Stephenson, West Ayton; MO, Michael Orr, Crathorne; MR, Malcolm Race, Great Ayton; RC, Robin Cook, Swainby; RFM, Ryedale Folk Museum, Hutton-le-Hole; WS, Walkers Studios, Scarborough.